-𝕬-
𝕳istory
OF THE
𝕮hurch
OF
𝕯urham

Simeon
of
Durham

A
HISTORY
OF
THE
CHURCH
OF
DURHAM

-

Translated
by
Joseph Stephenson.

ISBN 0947992162

Facsimile reprint published in 1988 by
Llanerch Enterprises,
Llanerch, Felinfach,
Lampeter, Dyfed.

Note: Simeon's account of
The Siege of Durhanm
is appended on page 97.

"Simeon's History of the Church of Durham" gives a detailed and connected account of the fortunes and migrations of the monks of St. Cuthbert, from the introduction of the Christian faith into Northumbria until the year 1096. Although professing to deal with ecclesiastical history only, it furnishes us with many important illustrations of the secular affairs of the northern districts of England. Simeon—for we have no longer any room to question its author—was well informed upon the incidents which he narrates, although it must be admitted that he is sometimes betrayed into serious errors. He loses no opportunity of magnifying the dignity and importance of his patron saint by recounting incidents which draw largely upon the credulity of his readers ; but these narratives for the most part so well illustrate either the history, or the manners, or the faith of the age to which they relate, that we are no losers by their introduction.

§ 12. Of this work there have appeared two editions. The first of these is contained in the collection of English historians known as Twysden's Decem Scriptores. It is formed upon two MSS., the Cottonian MS. Faustina A. v. (apparently contemporary with Simeon himself), the other in the public library of the University of Cambridge. This edition, although executed with considerable care, is now entirely superseded by the publication of Bedford's volume. which appeared in 1732. The great value of this later edition is, that it faithfully represents the text of a manuscript, (now belonging to the public library of the University of Durham,) which, as Rud has satisfactorily proved, is Simeon's autograph. With such an authority as this before us, supported by the Cottonian copy, Faustina A. v., any further reference to manuscripts becomes a work of supererogation. It is from this text that our translation has been made.

SIMEON'S HISTORY

OF THE CHURCH OF DURHAM.

HERE[1] begins the preface of Symeon, the reverend Monk and Precentor of the church of St. Cuthbert, of Durham, prefixed to his history of the origin of the Christian religion in the whole of Northumbria, and concerning the faith and lineage of the holy Oswald, king and martyr, and of the preaching of St. Aidan the bishop.

WHEN Oswald, that most Christian king, who was afterwards a martyr, was reigning over the Northumbrians, Aidan, a man of surpassing holiness, was the first who preached the word of faith in the realm of that sovereign, and was the earliest bishop of the church of Lindisfarne, or Durham; and, as that venerable priest and monk, Beda, tells us, in his History of the English,[2] he was the original founder of a residence for a bishop and monks in that church, at the command and by the assistance of this same king, in the year six hundred and thirty-five from our Lord's incarnation. From this mother church originated all the churches and monasteries of the province of the Bernicians; for the region of the Northumbrians is divided into two provinces, those of the Bernicians and Deirans. In this said church there continued for two hundred and forty years a noble and religious body of monks; but, about this time, a savage band of barbarians crossed the sea in countless vessels, and having arrived in England, they devastated the country far and near, and did not spare from death even the kings, of whom there were at that time many in England, one of whom was the glorious martyr, Edmund. They plundered the provinces of the Northumbrians[3] with even greater ferocity; and so thoroughly did they devastate with fire and sword all the churches and all the monasteries, that, after their departure, scarcely a trace of Christianity remained behind them. Eardulf, the bishop of the said church, escaped with difficulty; he and a few followers, who had saved their lives by flight, carried away with them the uncorrupted body of the holy

---

[1] This title is derived from Twysden's edition; that which is prefixed to the Durham MS. is in a late hand, and is as follows: " A short summary of the condition of the church of Lindisfarne and Durham, from the time of Aidan to that of William Kariliphe." [2] See Beda, E. H. § 156.
[3] See the present work, chap. xxi.

confessor, Cuthbert. Some of the monks, however, who had remained, trusting to the veneration with which the place was regarded, were dragged out of the church, and some were drowned by the enemy in the sea; others were carried off prisoners; the limbs of some were cut off, others were cruelly tortured, and all died together. Such was the destruction of the monastic assembly which had been connected with the body of St. Cuthbert. Besides this, the bishop whom we have mentioned, and several of his successors, in consequence of the barbarians having secured the ascendency over this province for many years, were compelled to wander about hither and thither, carrying with them the treasure of that holy body, never having repose from the presence of the barbarians, and the sword which was hanging over them; until at length, upon the restoration of peace, it was brought to Durham,[1] in consequence of a revelation from heaven, where now it reposes.

The monks of the said church having been thus slaughtered, as we have described, the younger members who were among them, for the purpose of being trained up and instructed in their discipline, escaped as they best might from the hands of the enemy, and accompanied the body of St. Cuthbert. But when, in consequence of the unfavourable circumstances in which they were placed, the strict monastic discipline in which they had been reared became slackened, they loathed it so much that they followed the allurements of a laxer mode of life. Nor were there any to constrain them by ecclesiastical censures; for the worship of God had nearly died out upon the destruction of the monasteries and churches. They lived mere secular lives; they were the slaves of the body; they begat sons and daughters; and their descendants, who continued in possession of the church of Durham, lived in the same lax way, for neither did they know anything better than a life according to the flesh, nor did they wish to know anything better. They were styled clerks; but they did not prove themselves to be such, either by their dress or their conversation. They followed the rule of St. Benedict, it is true, so far as to sing the Psalms at the prescribed hours; but this was the only point in which they adhered to the tradition delivered to them by their fathers from primitive monasticism.

But when king William the elder had obtained possession of the kingdom of England, and when religion began to revive in churches and monasteries, one of the clergy of Liege, named Walcher,[2] was elevated to the bishopric of the church of Durham—a man of noble birth, but nobler still by his prudence and honourable conduct. When he perceived that his church was occupied by men who were neither clerks nor monks of his own order, he was greatly distressed; the more especially when he discovered that they refused either to adopt a stricter mode of life, or to assume the usages of ecclesiastics. Having read the History of the English, and the Life of St. Cuthbert, (both of which were written by the venerable Beda,) he discovered—as we have already stated—that a congregation of monks had been established there by Aidan, the first bishop of that

See chaps. xxxvi. and xxxvii.   [2]. See chap. liii.

church, and by king Oswald, and that they served God both before the episcopate of St. Cuthbert, and after his death, ministering beside his holy body, until—as has been already mentioned—the wickedness of the enemy had swept them all away. Determining, therefore, that he would restore the ancient service in the church, he prayed to God that He would prevent him in all his doings, and further him with his continual help. Not long after this, certain meek-spirited monks,[1] belonging to the southern parts of England, having been admonished from heaven that they should go upon a pilgrimage for God's service into the province of Northumberland, came to bishop Walcher, and entreated him that he would assign them a place within his bishopric, in which they might reside, and that he would permit them to associate with their number such persons—if there were any such—who might be willing to serve God along with themselves. The bishop, being rejoiced at this request, embraced them with affection, as if they had been sent to him by God; he thanked heaven for their arrival, and welcomed them kindly; and, despatching them to Jarrow and Wearmouth, two places within his bishopric, which had formerly been the habitations of holy men, he commanded that they should reside there, and associate with themselves as many as desired to serve God along with them, until buildings, the construction of which required both time and deliberation, should have been prepared for their reception; and that thus they who were monks should be brought into the more immediate vicinity of Cuthbert, the monk and bishop. They did as he had directed; and having rebuilt the ancient dwellings of the saints, several persons profited so far by their life and example, that, renouncing the world, they attached themselves to the originators of this design. The bishop rejoiced greatly hereat; for he hoped that it would be through them that holy religion should be restored to a locality in which he had found scarce any remnant of honesty or piety. In the meantime, the foundations of buildings fitted for the reception of the monks were laid near the walls of the church of Durham; but before they were finished, the bishop was cut off by a cruel death[2] inflicted by the hands of his own people.

He was succeeded in the episcopate by William,[3] who was acknowledged by all who knew him to be a man of the greatest prudence and forethought. It grieved him to the heart to see the place unprovided with the fitting ecclesiastical and monastic arrangements; and he discovered, by the examination of earlier documents, that this church had been first founded, and afterwards perfected, by the instrumentality of monks, that is to say, by Aidan the monk and bishop, and those other monks by whom he had been accompanied; but that, in consequence of the destruction of these persons by the pagans, the church had lapsed from its primitive service. He determined, therefore, by God's assistance, that the older state of things should be restored; and that he would complete what his predecessor had begun. He[4] addressed himself, in the first instance, to those persons whom he found in possession of

[1] See chap. lvi.   [2] See chap. lix.   [3] See chap. lx.   [4] See chap. lxi.

the church; desiring them to become either regular clerks or
monks, so that they might lead a life in subjection to some rule or
other.   But they refused both; for it was not an easy thing for
them to abandon habits in which they had grown old, and to accept
a new system.   The bishop then laid the whole matter before the
great king William, who forthwith transmitted an embassy to pope
Gregory the seventh of holy memory, acquainting him with what
the bishop had discovered in books with respect to the church, and
what he had seen as to its present condition: he wished, moreover,
to consult him about these and other matters.   When the bishop
had spoken only a few words respecting the sanctity of the holy
father Cuthbert, the king was perfectly satisfied as to the expediency of the entire arrangement; namely, that the monks whom
he had found at these two places in his bishopric, namely, Wearmouth and Jarrow, should be united near the body of the saint,
since the smallness of the see rendered the existence of three
monasteries impossible.   When this arrangement had been confirmed by apostolic authority, the king, the archbishops, and the
bishops were informed by the pope what his pleasure was respecting it.   The king was exceedingly rejoiced herewith, and in the
presence of the whole of the nobility of the realm, he commanded
the bishop to carry this object into effect with all possible speed.
He did so; for he summoned the monks (the number of whom
had now considerably increased, the Holy Spirit having collected
together those who had been dispersed abroad) from the places
which we have mentioned, and he translated them to Durham,[1]
where he inseparably bound them and their successors to the body
of the blessed Cuthbert, that they should profess their adherence
to the mode of life and conversation which had been established by
their ancestors.   And thus it was that he had not introduced a new
monastic order, but, by God's help, he restored the older one.

HERE[2] BEGINS THE APOLOGY OF SYMEON THE MONK.

HAVING been required by the authority of my elders to narrate
the origin of this church, (that is, the church of Durham,) I at
first thought that I should decline to obey the order, in consequence of my want of skill and experience; but, on the other
hand, confiding rather in my obedience to those who commanded
me than my own talents, I have applied myself to the task according to the best of my ability.   I have collected together, and put
into order, whatever I found scattered about in loose memoranda;
by which means, those persons who are more skilful than myself

[1] See chap. lii.
[2] The Durham MS. contains the following title, but written by a more recent
hand: "Here begins a Treatise concerning the Condition of the Church of Lindisfarne (or of Durham), according to the venerable Beda; which is followed by the
History of the Bishops of Durham."

may (if my words please them not) the more readily find the means of accomplishing what I have here attempted.[1]

It seems fitting, therefore, that a list should be given of the names of all the bishops of that church, from its first founder to him[2] who holds it at present; and let future scribes take care that they fail not in appending the names of those who shall come hereafter :—

Aidan.	Cutheard.
Finan.	Tilred.
Colman.	Wigred.
Tuda.	Uhtred.
Eata.	Sixhelm.
Cuthbert.	Aldred.
Eadbert.	Elfsig.
Eadfrid.	Aldhun.
Ethelwold.	Eadmund.
Kynewulf.	Eadred.
Higbald.	Egelric.
Ecgbert.	Egelwin.
Heathured.	Walcher.
Ecgred.	William.
Eanbert.	Ralph.[3]
Eardulf.	

Here follow in writing the names of those monks in this church who, to this time, have made profession before the incorruptible body of the most holy Cuthbert; and it is our earnest request that the careful diligence of future times will add to this, as to the previous list, the names of all such as, by the favour of Christ, shall hereafter make profession there.

And, besides this, we beseech the reader that he would pray to our Lord Jesus Christ, both for him who commanded this work to be undertaken, and for those who, in obedience to that command, have brought it to completion. And lastly, that he be mindful to invoke the mercy of God upon all persons whose names he shall see here written; for the living, that here they may receive an increase of holy profession, and the reward of a good perseverance hereafter; and for the dead, that, having received the pardon of their offences, they may be permitted to see the goodness of the Lord in the land of the living.[4]

[1] Here in the MS. occurs a blank space, equivalent to about two lines.
[2] A slight erasure in the MS., the word "Ralph" having apparently been removed.
[3] This list is written in the hand of the scribe by whom the History was copied, but the names of subsequent occupants of the see have been added from time to time.
[4] Here, in the Durham MS., follows a long catalogue of the monks of Durham, which it has been considered unnecessary to repeat here.

HERE[1] BEGINS THE TREATISE CONCERNING THE ORIGIN AND
PROGRESS OF THIS CHURCH; THAT IS, THE CHURCH OF
DURHAM.

CHAP. I.—CONCERNING THE FAITH AND DESCENT OF ST. OSWALD, AND THE
PREACHING OF ST. AIDAN, WHO ARE THE CHIEF FOUNDATION-STONES OF THE
CHURCH OF DURHAM.

THIS holy church derives its original, both as regards its possessions and its religion, from the most fervent faith of Oswald,
that most illustrious king of the Northumbrians, and a most precious martyr; for, to the praise of God, it preserves within the safe
custody of our shrine, with inviolate care, those most sacred relics,
worthy of all veneration, the incorrupt body of the most holy
father, Cuthbert, and the adorable head of that king and martyr,
Oswald. For although the pressure of circumstances has removed
this church from the spot in which it was at the first established,
yet (by God's permission) it still retains its original character, which
it has derived from the constancy of its faith, from its dignity and
authority as an episcopal see, and from its adherence to the monastic
institutions which were herein established by king Oswald and
bishop Aidan. Since, then, it is our purpose to pen a truthful
narrative of the fortunes of this church, it is only fitting that we
should say a few words with respect to the hereditary nobility of
this sovereign, according to the flesh. For he was of an exceedingly
illustrious descent,—not only his father but his grandfathers were
kings; and of his brothers, two sat upon the throne, the one as his
predecessor, the other succeeded him. He was the son of that
most powerful king, Ethelfrid, whose father was Ethelric, whose
father again was Ida; and from Ida, as Beda[2] tells us, springs the
royal family of the Northumbrians. His pedigree was no less
illustrious on his mother's side than on his father's; for she was
the sister of king Edwin. But as these ancestors of his were unac-
quainted with the faith of Christ, he sprang up like a rose from out
of thorns; for not only was he regenerated to Christ in the sacred
font, but he lived a life most worthy of that holy regeneration.
When he succeeded to the throne, he forthwith subjugated himself
and his subjects to Christ; for he was an efficient companion and
assistant to bishop Aidan in the diffusion of the word of faith: for
while the bishop preached in his own language (that is to say, in
the Scottish tongue), this king, the devoted servant of the eternal
King, was in the habit of standing by and faithfully interpreting to
his nobles and attendants the words of truth; for he was as familiar
with the language in which the bishop spoke as with his own.
" The Ecclesiastical History of the English Nation,"[3] of which

---

[1] The title in the MS. is as follows: "A Chronicle respecting the Origin and
Progress of the Church of Durham, belonging to the registry, or office of the chan-
cery of the church of Durham."
[2] See Eccl. Hist. § 452, A. D. 547.   [3] Id. iii. 1, 2, etc.

Beda is the author, fully declares how illustrious a man this was, how great the devotion of his faith, how merciful and liberal to the poor, how earnestly attentive to prayer, even amidst the anxieties of a kingdom, and how glorious the many miracles which he wrought after his decease, in proof that he was at that time alive with Christ.

Here we are desirous to weave into one narrative, and to embody in one little book, as a memorial for posterity, the various incidents which are scattered throughout this work of Beda's, and in other treatises, so far as they illustrate the origin and the progress of this holy church of Durham. There are a few matters which, through a deficiency of historians, have not been committed to writing, and these we have resolved to append to our extracts from existing documents; our knowledge respecting them having been derived from the information of our trustworthy elders, who had either been eye-witnesses of these incidents, or had frequently heard them recounted by religious and credible personages, who themselves had personal knowledge of the same.

Chap. II.—As to the Year in which the blessed Oswald founded the Church of Lindisfarne, and that in which he died; and concerning the Episcopate of Aidan, and the Incorruptibility of the Arm of St. Oswald.

So, then, in the year of our Lord's incarnation six hundred and thirty-five (which is the one hundred and eighty-eighth year after the arrival of the Angles in Britain, and the thirty-ninth after that of St. Augustine,) the most pious king Oswald[1] appointed for Aidan, on his arrival, an episcopal see in the island of Lindisfarne, where that bishop commenced to erect a dwelling for the monks by whom he had been accompanied. In this he was acting in obedience to the king, who also assisted him herein; and thus, by the joint agency of the king and the bishop, the tender faith was confirmed by the pontifical authority, in order that it might for ever flourish and extend itself in a monastic institution. Hence, as we read, and have understood from the information of our elders, it was customary for monks to be elected to the episcopate of this church, after the example of Aidan, its first bishop, who was himself a monk, and one who, along with all his associates, led a life of monachism. This was observed from the year of our Lord's incarnation six hundred and thirty-five, until the year one thousand and seventy-two, when a religious man of the order of clerks, by name Gualcher,[2] a native of Lorraine, was ordained bishop; for I do not consider that that person[3] ought to be reckoned among the episcopate who, at an earlier period, had been ordained from among the clergy through the heresy of Simon: whom, however, death prevented from exercising any episcopal function. But (to return to my subject) Aidan, who was the first monk and bishop of that church, was himself a pattern to all monks and bishops who should

---

[1] See Beda, Eccl. Hist. § 155.
[2] See this present History, chap. lvii.   [3] Id. chap. xliv.

succeed him, pointing out to them the way of the Lord in which they ought to walk. After the venerable Beda[1] has detailed this man's most praiseworthy life, he adds : " And, that I may sum up much commendation in few words, I have to state—and my information is derived from those persons who were acquainted with him—his study was to neglect none of the duties which are inculcated in the gospels, or in the writings of the apostles or prophets, but to fulfil all of them to the utmost of his ability."

In the eighth year of the episcopate of Aidan, that most holy and devout king, Oswald, the earliest standard-bearer of the Christian faith in the whole nation of the Bernicians, and the founder of the church of Lindisfarne, from which every other church within the province derives its origin, fell in battle against the pagans, in the ninth year of his reign. His head was buried in the cemetery of the said church, but his arms and his hands (which the king by whom he was killed had ordered to be cut off) were buried in the royal city;[2] the right hand and arm continuing uncorrupt, according to the benedictional prayer of bishop Aidan; and it gives proof, even to our present age, by its preservation, of the merits of each of these two individuals, the king and the bishop.

This was frequently attested by a monk of our church (that is, of Durham), named Swartebrand, a man venerable from his grey hairs and his abundant simplicity of character, who was himself an eyewitness, and who died not long ago, during the episcopate of bishop William. For, as Beda[3] narrates, when the king was seated at table, upon the holy day of Easter, and there had just been placed before him a silver dish laden with kingly dainties, he was suddenly made aware that a great crowd of poor people were sitting in the streets, waiting for him to send them some alms ; whereupon he immediately commanded that the meat which had been set before him should be carried out to those poor people, and that the dish should be cut into pieces, and divided among them. Delighted with the kindness indicated by this action, the bishop, who was at the table, took hold of the king's hand, and exclaimed, " May this hand never grow old." His bones were translated to a monastery situated within the province of Lindsey.[4]

CHAP. III.—CONCERNING THE DEATH OF ST. AIDAN, THE DEPARTURE OF WHOSE SPIRIT WAS REVEALED TO THE EYES OF THE BLESSED CUTHBERT; AND AS TO THE PERIOD WHEN CUTHBERT ASSUMED THE HABIT OF A MONK.

AFTER having spent seventeen years in this episcopal see, bishop Aidan entered upon the way trodden by his fathers, and he was one of those to whom the death of the body opens a joyful entrance into another life. How great was the glory of his illustrious merits in the sight of Christ, is testified by the miracles by which he made himself conspicuous, both before and after his death ; as may be seen in the Third Book of the History to which we have already

---

[1] Eccl. Hist. § 162.   [2] Id. § 184.   [3] Id. § 166.   [4] Id. § 181.

referred. The most holy Cuthbert,[1]—that Israelite indeed, in whom
there was no guile,—being at that time living in the flesh, but not
after the flesh,—he, whose whole conversation from his childhood
was in heaven,—he, who in his youth imitated the life of an angel,
—was permitted to witness the holy and triumphal entrance of the
bishop into heaven, whither he was conducted by shining choirs
of rejoicing spirits. It happened that this future shepherd of souls
was at that time keeping a solitary watch among the mountains,
near the river Leder, over some cattle; and while he was spending
the night in prayer, his love and devotion carried him so wholly
heavenward, that he was deemed worthy of a glimpse of such
exceeding glory and brightness. Stimulated by this vision, the
youth beloved of God desired to attain a more exalted degree of
perfection, and to attain the glory of a reward which should place
him among the more renowned ones; and in the morning he
handed over to their owners the cattle which he had been tending,
and resolved that he would seek in a monastery a life of greater
perfection. It occurred in the year of our Lord's incarnation six
hundred and fifty-one, being the fifty-fifth since the arrival in
Britain of St. Augustine, the seventeenth year after the province of
the Bernicians had received the faith of Christ by the care of king
Oswald; and in this same year that bishop Aidan went to heaven,
(being the ninth year of the reign of king Oswin,) this most holy
youth, now dedicating himself to the service of Christ alone,
entered the monastery of Melrose, where he was received by that
most reverend abbot, Eata, whose attention had been directed
towards Cuthbert by Boisil. This Boisil was a man of great holiness, and one having the spirit of prophecy, who was then, in
subordination to the abbot, president of the monastery. Upon
being associated with the brethren, he showed forth (as Beda[2] tells
us in the book which his lucid pen has written concerning the life
of Cuthbert) who and what he was, how far his virtue was in
advance of the others, by his strict observance of the discipline
which is according to rule, by his earnestness in reading, labouring,
and watching, by his abstinence from every kind of intoxicating
drink, and by his devotedness to every work of piety. In short,
when he became a monk, he became a true monk,—a monk to be
respected, one in every particular worthy of praise, one who showed
by his soul and body, and dress, that he had joined the armies of
the Lord. In consequence of his inbred purity and religious disposition, the blessed Boisil loved him more than the others, and
instructed him in the knowledge of the Scriptures; as is evidenced
by the very book out of which the one instructed the other, a
volume preserved to this day in our church, and which, after so
many centuries, exhibits even at this present time a remarkable
freshness and beauty. When Boisil was translated to heaven,
Cuthbert succeeded his instructor in the office of provost; and by
his daily progress in virtue, he endeavoured to equal, or even to
surpass, his predecessor. If any one would wish to be informed as
to his diligence in calling all, by word and example, to heavenly

---

[1] See Beda's Life of St. Cuthbert, chap. iv.   [2] Id. § 11.

pursuits,—how illustrious he was by the splendour of his miracles, —how endowed with the grace of prophetic illumination,—let him read the book concerning his life, which we have already mentioned.

CHAP. IV.—CONCERNING BISHOP FINAN, HOW HE BAPTIZED THE KING OF THE MERCIANS, AND ORDAINED A BISHOP FOR THAT NATION; AND OF THE PROCEEDINGS OF CED, WHO WAS ORDAINED BY HIM.

FINAN succeeded Aidan in the bishopric; he was of the same nation and monastery as that from which his predecessor had been despatched. He built a church in the island of Lindisfarne, which was in keeping with his episcopal residence; and, at a later time, the most reverend archbishop Theodore dedicated it to the honour of the blessed apostle Peter; and Eadbert, the bishop of that place, (of whom more hereafter,) stripped off its covering of thatch, and carefully overlaid the whole of it, not only the roof but even the walls themselves, with sheets of lead. Penda,[1] the prince of the Midland Angles, was baptized by bishop Finan, in the province of the Northumbrians; and he returned home again with great joy, taking with him four priests, whose learning and previous life gave proof that they were well qualified to instruct and to baptize that nation.   Not long afterwards, Sigbert,[2] the king of the Eastern Saxons, received the washing of salvation at the hands of the same bishop; and thus, by the care of king Oswin and the conversion of king Sigbert, that province recovered the faith which it had formerly rejected when it had expelled bishop Mellitus;[3] and the word of Christ was preached therein by the priest Cedd, an Angle by descent, and a monk of the church of Lindisfarne, whom king Oswin had despatched thither for that very purpose; for he had on a former occasion preached the word, with much fruit, amongst the Midland Angles.   After he had thus gathered together to the Lord a large church in the province of the East Saxons, it happened that upon a certain occasion he returned to the church of Lindisfarne, to have a conference with bishop Finan; who, when he had understood how the work of the gospel had prospered in his hands, made him a bishop in the nation of the East Saxons, into which province he returned with his newly acquired dignity; and having collected an assemblage of the servants of Christ, both in the city which is called Ythancester,[4] and in that other named Tilaburg, (the former of which is situated upon the bank of the river Pente, the latter on that of the Thames,) in these he instructed them how to observe the discipline which a regular life requires.   He founded a third monastery also, in the province of the Northumbrians, in a place called Lestingaheu;[5] and the religious observances of this he conducted according to the rites of the inhabitants of Lindisfarne, in which he himself had been educated.   Upon his death, which occurred in this place, he entrusted its government to his brother Ceadda, who had himself been a monk of the church of Lindisfarne; for he had been one of Aidan's scholars.   Some time

[1] Beda, E. H. § 210.   [2] Id. § 213.   [3] Id. § 103.   [4] Id. § 214.   [5] Id. § 213.

after this, Ceadda was ordained bishop of the church of York, at the request of king Oswiu; and not long subsequently, archbishop Theodore ordered that he should preside over the province of the Mercians, and he fixed his episcopal see at a place called Licetfeld.

CHAP. V.—HOW COLMANN RESIGNED THE BISHOPRIC, AND OF THE DEATH OF TUDA, AND HOW HE PROCURED EATA FOR HIS SUCCESSOR.

FINAN having died in the tenth year of his episcopate, he was succeeded in the government of the church by Colmann, who had also been sent from Scotland. After he had spent three years in the episcopate, there arose a dispute about the keeping of Easter;[1] upon which he preferred to adhere to his national usages; and abandoning his see, he returned to his own country, in the thirtieth year after the Scots had entered upon the duties of the episcopate within the province of the Angles. How great was their moderation, how great their self-restraint, was proved by the place which he governed; for upon their departure very few houses were found; they had no property, saving only cattle; for if they received any sums of money from the rich they immediately distributed it among the poor. For there was no need to hoard up wealth, or to provide houses for the entertainment of the rich ones of this world; for they never resorted to the church except for the sole purpose of praying and hearing the word of God. For whenever, opportunity so requiring it, the king himself happened to come here, he was accompanied by not more than five or six attendants, and he departed as soon as his prayers were finished; and if they happened to take any refreshment, then they were contented with the frugal and daily fare of the brethren, and expected nothing more. For, at this time, the sole anxiety of those teachers was to serve God, not the world; their care was about the nourishment of the soul, not of the belly: and so entirely free were they from all taint of avarice, that no one accepted lands and possessions for the building of monasteries, unless constrained thereto by the powerful ones of the world; and this custom was for some time observed among the churches of the Northumbrians.

On his return home, Colmann took with him a portion of the bones of the most reverend father Aidan, part of them he left within the church over which he had ruled; and he commanded that they should be buried within the sacristy. Upon his return to his own country, Tuda, the servant of Christ, took the bishopric of the Northumbrians in his stead; he had been instructed and ordained bishop amongst the southern Scots. He was a good and a religious man; but a pestilence, which broke out and depopulated the province of the Northumbrians, cut him off that same year. Then the most reverend Eata, a man of exceeding gentleness, (who had been abbot in the monastery called Mailros,) was appointed as their abbot, to rule over such of the brethren as were content to

[1] Beda, E. H. § 226.

remain in the church of Lindisfarne, upon the departure of the
Scots; and it is reported that when Colmann was going away, he
asked and obtained this favour from King Oswiu, because Eata was
one of those twelve English youths whom Aidan, on his first arrival
in his episcopal see, had undertaken to instruct in Christianity; for
the king was exceedingly attached to this bishop Colmann, in
consequence of the prudence which he exhibited.

CHAP. VI.—As to the Time when Eata received the Bishopric, and when
  the blessed Cuthbert was converted, and to how great spiritual perfection he attained.

In the year six hundred and sixty-four from our Lord's incarnation, (being the thirtieth year after an episcopal see and a dwelling
for monks had been established in the island of Lindisfarne by
those most earnest worshippers of Christ, king Oswald and bishop
Aidan,) and in the same year in which the Scots had abandoned
the church and returned home, abbot Eata, as we have mentioned,
assumed the care of that church or monastery; and having done so,
he removed thither the blessed Cuthbert, who was now spending,
in the monastery of Melrose, the fourteenth year of his life, after
having become a monk.   Eata's object in so doing was this; that
Cuthbert should instruct the brethren of Lindisfarne how to observe
the regular discipline, as well by his authority, since he was their
provost, as by the example of his virtuous life.   The venerable
priest and monk Beda[1] has stated, in the book which he has
written concerning the life and miracles of that same father Cuthbert, why that place was formerly under the rule of bishops, and
then under that of an abbot; and also how it happened that the
custom originated of choosing bishops to the care of this church
rather from amongst the order of monks than of clerks. His words
are these: " Let no one be surprised, that in this same little island
of Lindisfarne, we have stated that there is a residence for a bishop
as well as for an abbot and monks; for such indeed is the truth.
One and the same residence shelters both these servants of God at
one and the same time ; yea, it affords a residence for all the monks.
For Aidan, who was the first bishop of this place, was also a monk,
and his invariable usage was to observe a monastic life in every
respect, as did all his followers; and hence it is that even to this
present day all the rulers of that place execute the office of a bishop
in such manner as that, whilst the monastery is under the rule of
an abbot, (whom they elect, with the advice of the brethren,) all the
priests, deacons, chanters, readers, and all other ecclesiastics of every
grade, observe the monastic rule along with the bishop." But upon
this head we have said enough.
     When Cuthbert, that man of God, had arrived at the church or
monastery of Lindisfarne, he lost no time in communicating to the
brethren the rules of monastic discipline, as well by his instructions

---

[1] See the Life of St. Cuthbert, § 25.

as by his mode of life; and, as was his usual custom, he stimulated, by his frequent visits, the people who resided in his neighbourhood to seek after and prepare themselves for the joys of heaven. Having become celebrated by his power in working miracles, he, by his continued prayers, restored to their former health many who were afflicted with various diseases and torments; he cured many who were vexed by evil spirits ; and this he did not only when present, by his prayers, his touch, his commands, or his exorcisms, but even when absent his prayers sufficed for the purpose ; and even sometimes nothing more than the announcement that they would be cured brought the cure.   There were in the monastery some of the brethren who would have preferred obeying their earlier customs rather than the discipline which is according to rule, but these he overcame by the modest power of his patience ; and by daily exercises he led them to adopt, little by little, that estate of higher promise.   He was conspicuous from his patience, he was unconquered in his steady endurance of every adversity which could afflict either the mind or the body ; no less did he exhibit a cheerful countenance in the midst of calamities ; so that it might be clearly seen that he was a man whom the internal consolations of the Holy Spirit enabled to be victorious over external pressure.   By these and such like spiritual exercises, not only did this venerable personage excite all good men to imitate him, but further, by the regularity of his life, he recalled from their obstinacy in error those who had been living in sin and rebellion.   Let those who wish to know him read his life, and they will discover that the abundant grace of the Holy Spirit filled to overflowing this vessel with every virtue ; let them learn, by the precedent of this man, the respective duties of submission and authority, the excellence of justice and piety, how to temper gentleness with severity ; all these duties, I repeat, they may learn from his example.   Let those monks, who now serve him, learn how to be in subjection to those who have the rule over them,—learn obedience, love, reverence, and all submission, in purity of heart.   And let all those who are his successors in the duty of government, learn from his example how to overcome the injuries of their opponents by the modest virtue of patience ; let them discover how to reprove transgressors by the fervency of their zeal for justice, and in the spirit of meekness to be gentle in the pardoning of the penitent.   For when the transgressors were confessing their sins to him, he was the first to shed tears in his sorrow for their weaknesses; and he showed them, by his own example, though he were guiltless, what course ought to be adopted by the sinner.   None left him without having tasted of the joys of consolation, none carried away the sorrow with which he had been oppressed when he sought an interview.

CHAP. VII.—AT WHAT TIME THE BLESSED CUTHBERT ACCEPTED THE PRIORATE OF THE CHURCH OF LINDISFARNE; AND HOW HE WAS DELIGHTED WITH THE LIFE OF AN ANCHORITE.

IN the year six hundred and seventy-six after the incarnation of our Lord, (which is the sixth year of the reign of king Ecgfrid,) when Cuthbert, the man of the Lord, had spent more than twelve years as prior over the monastery of Lindisfarne, he withdrew himself into the private seclusion of an anchorite's life, having obtained the permission of his prior and the brethren ; striving there, as elsewhere, to advance from good to become better, and from better best. There thou, O sweetest father, wast so much nearer God as thou wast further from the world and its clamorous anxieties; there thou, O most holy and most revered, along with Mary didst sit at the feet of the Lord, having chosen that better part which shall be thine for ever. There thy thirsting soul desired access to God, the Fountain of living waters, and fainted for the courts of the Lord's house; there thy flesh and thy heart rejoiced in the living God, and thou didst taste and see how sweet the Lord was, and·thou wast blessed, because thy hope was in Him. With what earnestness, with how many sighs of love, with what affection, with what repentance, and with how many tears, didst thou wish, and ask, and entreat, and exclaim with the prophet, "Lord, I have loved the habitation of thine house, and the place where thine honour dwelleth" (Ps. xxvi. 8). For, setting aside all other desires, his whole life expressed only this prayer, "One thing have I sought of the Lord, which I will require; even that I may dwell in the house of the Lord all the days of my life" (Ps. xxvii. 4). And so thou, blessed among the blessed, didst dwell in the house of the Lord; and thou shalt praise him for ever and ever.

The spot in which the servant of the Lord obtained such privileges is the island of Farne, which is surrounded on the one side by a deep sea, on the other by the boundless ocean ; at that time it produced no water whatever, nor tree, nor corn ; and it was unfitted for the residence of mankind, for it was the habitation of evil spirits. Miracles accompanied the holy man even thither; his prayers called a well out of the stony rock, he obtained a crop of corn from the hard earth ; and, having expelled the old enemy and his attendants, the place became fitted for the abode of man. For after this temple of the Holy Spirit took up his residence in this island, the evil spirit so hated that locality, that the servant of Christ, during the period of his abode in it, experienced no annoyance from the illusions of devils.

CHAP. VIII.—AS TO THE TIME AT WHICH THE HOLY BEDA WAS BORN, AND ABOUT HIS MONASTERY; AND HOW REMARKABLE ENGLAND WAS AT THIS PERIOD FOR LEARNING.

IN the second year which this most holy father spent in a life of solitude, (that is, the year six hundred and seventy-seven from the incarnation, and the seventh of the reign of king Ecgfrid, and the

ninth after the arrival of archbishop Theodore in Britain,) Beda was
born, in the province of the Northumbrians, in the property belonging to the monastery of the apostles Peter and Paul, which is at
Wearmouth and Jarrow. When he was seven years of age, he was
entrusted by his relations to the care of the most reverend abbot
Benedict, and afterwards to Ceolfrid, that he might be educated ;
and this occurred in the tenth year after the foundation of that
same monastery of St. Peter the Apostle, and the third after the
commencement of the monastery of St. Paul. So great was the
agreement and affection which existed between these two monasteries, so close the bond of concord and brotherly love by which
they were united, that (as Beda[1] himself afterwards describes it)
they might be regarded as one monastery located in two separate
places. Hence it is that when he mentions it, in his History of the
Angles,[2] he speaks of them as one ; " The monastery of Peter and
Paul, situated at the mouth of the river Wear, and near the river
Tyne, at a place called Jarrow." Here that youth of good hope was
carefully instructed in divine and secular learning, in order that he
should become the organ of the Holy Spirit, by Whom his mind was
so illuminated for the strengthening of the holy catholic church,
that he was to be the author of many books of commentaries upon
the Old and New Testaments. After he had been instructed in
the Latin tongue, he attained no mean skill in that of Greece ; for
he was a student in that monastery at the time when archbishop
Theodore and abbot Adrian—men thoroughly acquainted with
secular and ecclesiastical literature—visited the whole of Britain ;
and having collected together a crowd of disciples, instructed them
daily in useful knowledge, so that their hearers were made acquainted with the rules of metre, astronomy, and ecclesiastical
calculation, as well as the Holy Scriptures. This we learn from
Beda[3] himself, who immediately afterwards adds : " In proof of
this, there remain, even to the present day, some of their scholars,
to whom the Latin and Greek languages are as familiar as their own
native tongue." When father Cuthbert departed to the heavenly
country, Beda, the future historian of his life, at this time in his
eleventh year, had now devoted four years to study in the monastery ; but as we shall have an opportunity, ere long, of speaking of
him more fully, we shall now return to the point from which our
narrative diverged.

CHAP. IX.—CONCERNING THE ELECTION OF ST. CUTHBERT, AND HOW HE WAS
INDUCED TO LEAVE FARNE; AND WHERE HE WAS CONSECRATED, AND OF THE
GIFTS GIVEN TO HIM UPON THAT OCCASION BY KING EGFRID.

IN the year of our Lord's incarnation six hundred and seventy-
eight, (being the eighth year of the reign of king Ecgfrid,) a dispute
originated between that king and Wilfrid, who for no short time
had administered the episcopate of the whole province of the

[1] See Life of the abbot Benedict, § 7.
[2] See §§ 427, 458, and the present History chap. xiii.
[3] See Eccl. Hist. § 256.

Northumbrians; in consequence of which he was driven from his
bishopric, and in his stead two bishops were ordained at York, by
archbishop Theodore, for the government of the nation of the
Northumbrians; namely, Bosa, who was to preside over the province of Deira, and the abbot Eata, (whom we have frequently
mentioned,) for the province of the Bernicians.   The former fixed
his episcopal residence at the city of York, the latter at the church
of Hexham and Lindisfarne; and both of them had been monks
before they attained the rank of the bishopric.   After Eata had
presided over the church of Lindisfarne as its abbot for fourteen
years, he assumed the government of these two churches, in the
third year after father Cuthbert had entered upon the solitude of
his hermit's residence.   Three years after the departure of Wilfrid,
Theodore ordained Tunbert to the church of Hexham; while for
four years Eata continued in the government of the church of
Lindisfarne.

After the lapse of these four years, it so happened that a large
synod was congregated, under the presidency of archbishop Theodore of blessed memory, and in the presence of the most pious and
God-beloved king Egfrid, at a place called Twiford (which means
The double ford), near the river Alne; where, by the unanimous consent of all, the blessed father Cuthbert was chosen to the bishopric
of the church of Lindisfarne.   When he refused to be withdrawn
from his seclusion, even after many messengers and letters had
been despatched for the purpose, at length the king himself, accompanied by the most holy bishop Trumwine, and many other
ecclesiastics and noblemen, sailed to the island.   Several of the
brethren came thither from the isle of Lindisfarne, for the same
purpose.   They all knelt down, and they adjured him by the Lord,
they wept and prayed, until they carried him off to the synod; he
also weeping while he abandoned his beloved retreat.   On his
arrival there, the united wishes of the assembly overcame his
repugnance, and he was compelled to bend his neck so as to accept
the office of a bishop; induced thereto chiefly by the words of
Boisil, the servant of the Lord, who, with a prophetic mind, had
foretold him all that should come to pass, and had predicted that
he should become a bishop.   However, he was not at once ordained; but the winter, then close at hand, was allowed to pass
over.   Thus, after he had dedicated to God nine years of a life of
solitude, he was, by His good pleasure, elevated to the honour of
the bishophood, being consecrated at York, on the seventh of the
kalends of April [26th March], in the year of our Lord six hundred
and eighty-five, on Easter-day, in the presence of king Ecgfrid, in the
twelfth year of that sovereign's reign.   Seven bishops met together
for his consecration, the chief of whom was archbishop Theodore
of blessed memory, by whom also the office of ordination was performed.   He was at the first elected to the bishopric of the church
of Hexham, in the room of Tunbert, who had been deposed from
that diocese; but, because he much preferred the church of Lindisfarne, in which he had resided, it was arranged that Eata should
return to this his see in the church of Hexham, over which he had

been ordained at the first, and that Cuthbert should undertake the government of the church of Lindisfarne. The said king and Theodore gave him the whole land in the city of York which extends from the wall of the church of St. Peter, as far as the great gate towards the west, and from the wall of that church, as far as the city wall upon the south ; they gave him also the vill of Craik, with a circuit of three miles around it, that he might have a dwelling in which to rest on his way to York, or on his return thence. There he appointed a residence for monks ; but because this land was inadequate for the purpose, he received as an augmentation, Lugubalia, (which is called Luel,) embracing a circuit of fifteen miles, where he also established a congregation of nuns, and consecrated the queen, to whom he had given a religious garb ; here also he founded schools for the improvement of divine service. Other landed possessions also were assigned to him, which it would be tedious to specify; nor is this necessary, since they are recorded in the writings belonging to the church. But in the same year in which king Ecgfrid had caused this venerable father to be ordained bishop, he was killed at Nechtanesmere (that is, The lake of Nechtan), along with a large portion of the troops which he had taken with him to plunder the land of the Picts. This happened, as the same father Cuthbert had predicted, upon the thirteenth of the kalends of June [20th May], in the fifteenth year of his reign. His body was buried in Iona, the island of Columba.

CHAP. X.—How CUTHBERT LIVED WHILE HE WAS BISHOP; AND HOW HE DEPARTED FROM THE WORLD, AND HOW HE PERMITTED HIMSELF TO BE CARRIED BACK TO THE CHURCH OF LINDISFARNE.

IMITATING the blessed apostles, the venerable Cuthbert adorned with good works the episcopal office which he had assumed; for by his continual prayers he protected the people committed to his charge, and called them to mind the things of heaven by his wholesome exhortations. Moreover, the things which he said ought to be done, these he himself did ; a thing to which all teachers should give heed. Just as at an earlier period he had given an example of obedience and humility to inferiors by his own submission to his spiritual father, and when as provost had exhibited in himself the pattern of how the provost of a monastery should exercise authority, so now that he had become a bishop, he left behind him an example of what should be the life of a bishop. Therefore, let those who follow him in this exalted position, study how they may also follow his life, that, by a conversation worthy of such a predecessor, they may become, like him, well pleasing to God. Let them carefully contrast, on the one hand, his mode of life—on the other, their own ; let them look into this matter carefully, I repeat, that they, laden with their sins, sit not down in that see which he rendered glorious and renowned by the splendour of every virtue. To adopt the language which the church employs when she celebrates his praise, thanking God for him, he shone, forth as an illustrious personification of every virtue, in angelic chastity, in prophetic dignity, in apostolic virtue. He was chiefly noted for the fervency of his love towards God, for his modest patience, for the earnest devotion of his unceasing prayers, for his affability to all who came to him for the sake of comfort; for he counted that if he were employed in affording the aid of his exhortation to the weaker brethren, this was no less acceptable than prayer to God; for He who has commanded, "Thou shalt love the Lord thy God," has also said, "Thou shalt love thy neighbour." He was remarkable for self-severity by means of fasting; he was ever intent upon heavenly matters through the grace of repentance. And, lastly, when he offered to God the sacrifice of the health-giving victim, he did not elevate his voice, but tearfully put up his prayers to the Lord from the bottom of his heart.

After having spent two years in the episcopate, he returned to his island and monastery; and, shortly after the holy festival of our Lord's Nativity, he was warned from above that the day of his death was at hand, or rather of his entrance into that life which alone is worthy of the name of life. After having spent nearly two months in the enjoyment of the quiet which he had recovered, he was seized with a sudden disease, and the presence of temporal pain began to prepare him for the joys of perpetual blessedness. During three weeks he was unceasingly afflicted with a disease which at length brought him to his end. His sickness began upon the fourth day of the week, and again, on the fourth day of the week his sickness ended, and he departed to the Lord. During his illness he sent this message by Herefrid, a priest of devout religion, who at this time governed the monastery of Lindisfarne as abbot, saying: "When God shall have taken my soul, bury me in this my dwelling, near the place in which I used to pray, towards the south, and on the eastern side of the holy cross which I have there erected. On the north of the said oratory there is a coffin hidden under the turf, which was given me some time ago by the venerable abbot Cudda; after you have wrapped my corpse in the linen cloth which you will find here, deposit it in the same coffin. Whilst I was alive, I refused to wear it; but out of my affection for the abbess Verca, that woman beloved of God, who sent it to me, I carefully preserved it, in order that my dead body might be shrouded therein." But when the brethren entreated him that he would permit his corpse to be removed to the church of Lindisfarne, for interment there, he added: "My wish certainly was that here I should rest in the body, for here it is that I have fought my little warfare for the Lord; here I desire to finish my course; it is from this spot that the merciful Judge will remove me to receive (as I hope) the crown of justice; and even for your own sakes, I think it will be more expedient that I should repose here, that thus you may escape the visits of fugitives and criminals, who would probably flock to the burial-place of my body; for, mean as I am, there has gone abroad the report that I am the servant of God, and therefore you would very frequently find it necessary to intercede for such characters as

these with the secular authorities; so that the presence of my
body would be productive of much trouble to you." But when the
brethren had been instant with many and long-continued entreaties,
and had urged in reply that this labour would be easily borne by
them, and would even be acceptable, the man of God at length
answered, after deliberation : " If you are determined to overrule
my arrangements, and to carry back my remains thither, it appears
to me to be very expedient that you should bring my corpse within
your church, so that you can visit my sepulchre when you please ;
and it will be in your own power to decide which of those persons
who come shall be admitted." The brethren knelt upon the ground,
and thanked him for the permission and the advice which he had
given them ; and for this permission and advice we also render
our thanks, not only upon bended knees, but also with the whole
body, and with hearts bowed down before him. We, I say, offer
him our thanks ; for he has permitted us, though unworthy, to see
his uncorrupted body, and to handle it with our hands, four hundred
and eighteen years [1] after his decease. Let us return thanks to
St. Cuthbert, and let us, out of our love towards him, think it
a light and pleasant task to defend those who flee to his sepulchre
for protection ; and let us consider as trifling and unimportant any
adversity brought upon us by this present uncertain world, so long
as we rejoice in having in our possession that inestimable treasure
of his holy body.

But now when he saw, from the progress of the disease, that the
time of his dissolution was at hand, he bequeathed to his brethren
who survived him this address as their inheritance ; and he thus
bade them farewell, speaking to them a few words, but effective ones,
respecting peace and humility, and how they should shun those
persons who rather strove against peace than for it. " Keep peace,"
said he, " one with another always, and the love of God ; and when
need demands that you deliberate as to your estate, take great care
that you be of one mind in your decisions." And he subjoined
those other exhortations for the preservation of faith and love, and
for the observance of the life which is according to rule, which are
to be seen in his biography.[2] When the usual period had arrived
for the offering up of the nightly prayer, he fortified his departure by
receiving the wholesome sacraments ; and, having raised up his
eyes to heaven and stretched out his hands, he breathed forth his
soul, which had so long been occupied in the contemplation of the
praises and the joys of heaven. Thus he died, in the year six hundred and eighty-seven, after having spent two years in the bishopric;
fifty-three years after king Oswald and Aidan had established an
episcopal see and a residence for monks in the said island ; in the
thirty-eighth year after he had assumed the monastic dress at
Mailros, although even from his childhood he had always lived like
a monk, both in theory and practice.

The brethren placed the venerable body of the father in a ship,

---

[1] This circumstance, indicating the year 1105, is one of the chronological data
which are of importance in deciding the period at which this work was written,
and its author.   [2] That is, in § 65.

and conveyed it to the island of Lindisfarne, where it was received by a great multitude of people who met it, together with choirs of choristers; and it was deposited in a stone coffin, at the right side of the altar, in the church of the blessed Peter the Apostle. But after the man of God was buried, so violent was the storm of trial which shook that church, that many of the brethren chose rather to depart from the place than to encounter such perils; while the affairs of the see were for that year managed by the venerable bishop Wilfrid, until a successor for Cuthbert should be elected and ordained.

In the following year[1] Eadbert was ordained bishop, a man noted for his acquaintance with the divine Scriptures, and for his observance of the heavenly precepts, but more especially for works of alms-giving; so much so, that according to the law, he every year paid the tithe, not only of his fourfooted stock, but also of all his corn and fruit; and he also gave a part of his garments to the poor. And when he was elevated to the see the tempest of the disturbance, to which we have already alluded, was dispelled, just as is expressed by the Scripture, "The Lord doth build up Jerusalem" (that is, The vision of peace), "and gather together the outcasts of Israel; He healeth those that are broken in heart, and giveth medicine to heal their sickness." [Ps. cxlvii. 3.]

CHAP. XI.—How, AFTER HIS BODY HAD BEEN BURIED FOR ELEVEN YEARS, IT WAS FOUND UNCORRUPT; AND CONCERNING BISHOP EADBALD, AND ETHELWOLD, BOTH OF WHOM SUCCEEDED HIM IN HIS CELL; AND AT WHAT TIME BEDA WROTE HIS LIFE.

WHEN eleven[2] years had passed since the period of his death, the brethren opened his tomb, and found his corpse quite as fresh as if he had recently been buried. The limbs were flexible, and his whole appearance was more like that of a man who was asleep than of one dead: the vestments also in which he was clothed not only were entire, but they exhibited as marvellous a freshness and glossiness as they had done when they were new. Seeing this, the brethren were immediately struck with such great fear and trembling that they scarce dared to speak, scarce to look upon the miracle which was revealed to them, scarce did they know what to do. But removing a small portion of the garments, thirsting to give proof of their incorruption, (for they did not venture to touch those which were near his flesh,) they hurried away to make the bishop acquainted with the discovery. He gladly received the gifts, and joyfully heard their account of the miracle; and with devout affection did he kiss the garments, as if they were yet surrounding the body of the father. "Gird," he said, "his body with fresh wrappings in the stead of those which you have removed, and then replace him in the shrine which you have prepared; for I am perfectly aware that this place, which has been consecrated by so great a miracle from heaven, shall not long remain empty; and truly

---

[1] A.D. 688.   [2] A.D. 698.

blessed is the man to whom the Lord, the Author and Giver of all blessedness, shall grant the privilege of resting therein." When the bishop had uttered such words as these, and more than these, accompanied by many tears, with great compunction, and with a trembling tongue, the brethren did as he commanded them; and having wrapped the body in new raiment and placed it in a new shrine, they deposited it, with the reverence to which it was entitled, upon the pavement of the sanctuary. But the brethren took a portion of his hair, that they might have something to give, as a relic, to such of his friends as asked for the same, or show in proof of the miracle.

Shortly after this the bishop beloved of God, Eadbert, was attacked with a sore disease, and the sharpness of the disorder gaining strength day by day, not long afterwards, that is to say, on the day before the nones of May [6th May[1]], he also departed to the Lord, having obtained from Him the gift for which he had been such an earnest suppliant; namely, that he might leave the body, not snatched away by a sudden death, but after having been refined by a long sickness. When they placed his corpse in the tomb of the blessed father Cuthbert, they deposited it upon the top of the coffin in which they had enshrined the uncorrupted members of that father.

Beda, in pure and simple diction, narrates the history of this blessed Cuthbert—the commencement, the progress, and the end of his most glorious conversation—exactly as he had ascertained the particulars thereof from the indisputable testimony of those brethren who had lived along with him: for God's mercy had provided that one whose authority was so widely recognised throughout the whole catholic church should be the writer of the angelic life of an individual who resided in this remote corner of the world. It is satisfactory then, God so disposing it, that the bones of that writer who narrated for the satisfaction of future ages the pious labours undertaken for Christ's sake, and also the fact of incorruption of St. Cuthbert after he had been buried eleven years, should now, at length,[2] repose along with the bones of that deceased father. After the death of father Cuthbert, Wilfrid (as we have already mentioned[3]) held the episcopate of his church for a single year; for at this time he had recovered his see and episcopate by the invitation of king Aldfrid, who was at that time reigning after his brother Ecgfrid. The church was now ruled by these holy bishops, Eadbert for ten years, and after him Eadfrid for twenty-four, both of whom were men beloved of God. In the time of this Eadfrid, Beda, being then in the thirtieth year of his age, and having now received the rank of the priesthood, began to write his books, in the composition of which he laboured with unceasing diligence for twenty-nine years, that is, until the close of his life, meditating day and night in the law of the Lord. Among others,

---

[1] A.D. 698; see Eccl. Hist. § 254.

[2] It will be remembered that the remains of St. Cuthbert and the venerable Beda were deposited in the church of Durham. For an account of the proceedings by which this was accomplished, see chap. xli.   [3] See the previous chapter

he wrote the book of the life of father Cuthbert, to which we
have alluded so frequently, in which he thus addresses the said
bishop : [1]—

"To the holy lord and the most blessed father, bishop Eadfrid,
and to all the congregation of the brethren who serve Christ in the
island of Lindisfarne, your faithful fellow-servant Beda sendeth
greeting.   Since, brethren most beloved, it is your pleasure that I
should prefix a preface, as is usual, to the book which I have composed at your request respecting the life of our father Cuthbert
of blessed memory,"—the remainder of which letter you may see
in the preface itself, as it is prefixed to that treatise.   And as he is
about to recount the benefits conferred by Cuthbert upon others,
he first of all narrates a miracle wrought upon himself ; how his
tongue was healed while he was singing the praises of the saint, as
he himself tells us in the letter [2] addressed to John the presbyter,
which he prefixed to the metrical life of St. Cuthbert, of which he
also is the author.

Thus the most reverend bishop Eadfrid, in the proving of his
love for his predecessor, the blessed Cuthbert, restored from its
foundations the oratory which that father had erected in the island
in which he had lived a hermit's life, and which had now become
ruinous from age, and which at this time was occupied by the
anchorite Felgild, who therein had succeeded Aethelwold.   This
latter individual, after having spent many years in the monastery
called In Hripum, and having adorned by his actions the office
of the priesthood which he had received, succeeded that man of
God, Cuthbert, in living the life of a recluse upon the island of
Farne, where he continued twelve years, and in which he died ;
but he was buried in the island of Lindisfarne, near the bodies of
the bishops whom we have mentioned, in the church of the blessed
apostle Peter.

CHAP. XII.—CONCERNING BISHOP ETHELWOLD, AND THE CROSS OF STONE WHICH
HE MADE.

UPON the death of bishop Eadfrid, that priest of religious life,
Aethelwold, the abbot of the monastery of Melrose, succeeded his
predecessors in the bishopric ; and he held the see for sixteen
years with honour to it and to himself.   The life [3] of the blessed
father Cuthbert tells us, that before this man attained to the government of this monastery as its abbot, he was the worthy attendant
upon the saint.   He it was who caused a stone cross of curious
workmanship to be made, and directed that his own name should be
engraven upon it, as a memorial of himself, the top of which was
broken off by the pagans when they devastated the church of Lindisfarne at a later period ; but it was afterwards reunited to the
body of the cross by being run together with lead, and subsequently
to this it was constantly carried about along with the body of St.

---

[1] In the present series, i. 546.
[2] A translation of this letter will be found along with the other portions of
Beda's correspondence.   [3] § 77.

Cuthbert, and honourably regarded by the people of Northumbria out of regard to these two holy men. And at the present day it stands erect in the cemetery of this church (that is, the church of Durham) and exhibits to all who look upon it a memorial of these two bishops, Cuthbert and Ethelwold.

CHAP. XIII.—CONCERNING THE FAMILY OF KING CEOLWULF, AND OF HIS LIFE AND PATIENCE.

IN the year of our Lord's incarnation seven hundred and twenty-nine, being the fifth of the pontificate of Aethelwold, Osric king of the Northumbrians, the son of king Aldfrid, departed from this life, having appointed as his successor Ceolwulf, the brother of king Coenred, who had filled the throne before himself. This Ceolwulf was, it is true, of the family of Ida the first king of the Northumbrians, but he did not trace his pedigree through his son king Aethelric, from whom those glorious kings Oswald and Oswin derived their descent. Ceolwulf's genealogy[1] sprang from a brother of Aethelric, named Ocga; for he was the son of Cutha, whose father was Cuthwine, whose father was Liodwald, whose father was Ecgwald, whose father was Aldhelm, whose father was Ocga, whose father was Ida. Ida had twelve sons, from whom descended the kings of the Northumbrians; their names were Addas, Ethelric, Theodric, Edric, Theudheri, Osmer, Alric, Ecga, Osbald, Scor, Sceotheri, and Ocga, from whom descended two brothers, Coenred and Ceolwulf, both of whom were kings.

The commencement and progress of the reign of this Ceolwulf were marked by a continued succession of misfortunes, but afterwards, when peace and tranquillity smiled upon him, many of the Northumbrians, as well nobles as private individuals, laid aside their arms, and having accepted the tonsure, gave the preference to a monastic life over that spent in warlike occupations. As we shall hereafter[2] state more fully, the king himself was one of these. He was devoted to liberal studies, and he is celebrated by Beda for his diligence in reading and hearing the holy Scriptures and the history of earlier ages. · In the dedication to the history of the English nation, inscribed to that sovereign, occurs the following passage : " To the most illustrious king Ceolwulf, Beda, the servant of Christ, and presbyter, sends greeting. I formerly, at your request, had the greatest satisfaction in transmitting to you the Ecclesiastical History of the English nation, which I had lately published, in order that you might at that time read it and give it your approval; and now I send it to you, the second time, that you may cause it to be transcribed, and now read it more at your leisure. And I cannot but commend the sincerity and zeal with which you not only give diligent attention · to the hearing of the words of holy Scripture, but also industriously take care how you may become acquainted with the actions and sayings of former men of renown, more especially those of our own nation."

[1] See the Saxon Chron. A.D. 731, and Florence, p. 389.
[2] See chap. xvi.

CHAP. XIV.—As to the Period at which the holy Beda died, how he
lived, and what he wrote.

In the year of our Lord's incarnation seven hundred and thirty-
five, being the seventh year of the reign of king Ceolwulf, and the
eleventh of the episcopate of Aethelwold, died that writer of holy
books, the venerable priest and monk Beda, in the fifty-ninth year
of his age. That lamp of the universal church now returned to
the Father of lights ; that rill of water springing up into eternal
life was restored to God, the living Fountain. At this time one
hundred and one years had elapsed from the period at which king
Oswald and bishop Aidan had appointed, in the island of Lindisfarne, an episcopal see and a dwelling-place for the monks ; it was
sixty-two years from the building of the monastery of St. Peter
the Apostle at Wearmouth, and forty-nine from the decease of father
Cuthbert. During his lifetime this Beda lay hidden within a
remote corner of the world, but after his death his writings gave
him a living reputation over every portion of the globe. It might
here be thought—so accurate are the details of his description of
them—that he had personally visited the several countries respecting which he has written, and familiarised himself with their varied
peculiarities; yet he spent the whole of his life within the monastery
in which he was educated, from his infancy even to the day on
which he was called away from this present life. In order to
remove all hesitation as to our accuracy on this point, it has been
thought expedient to introduce here his own description of himself.
His words are these :

   " I, Beda, the servant of Christ, and a presbyter of the
monastery of the blessed apostles Peter and Paul, which is at
Wearmouth and Jarrow, was born within the territory of the same
monastery. When I was seven years old, I was consigned by the
care of my relatives to the most reverend abbot Benedict, in
order that I might be educated by him, and afterwards by Ceolfrid ;
and from that period, spending all the remaining time of my life
within that monastery, I devoted myself wholly to the study of
the Scriptures ; and amidst the observance of the discipline prescribed by our rule, and the daily duty of singing in the church,
my constant delight was either in learning, or teaching, or writing.
In the nineteenth year of my age I received deacon's orders ;
those of the priesthood in my thirtieth year ; both of them
were conferred through the ministry of the most reverend bishop
John, and by order of the abbot Ceolfrid. From the period at
which I received priest's orders until my fifty-ninth year, I have
made it my business, for the use of me and mine, briefly to com-
pile out of the works of the venerable fathers, and to interpret and
explain, according to their meaning, (adding, however, somewhat of
my own,) the following treatises :—

   " On the Beginning of Genesis, as far as the Nativity of Isaac,
and the Casting-out of Ishmael, four books.

   " Of the Tabernacle and its Vessels, and of the Vestments of the
Priests, three books.

" Of the First Part of Samuel, that is, to the Death of Saul, four books.

" Of the Building of the Temple, two books of Allegorical Exposition, like the rest.

" Also, on the Book of Kings, thirty Questions.

" Upon the Proverbs of Solomon, three books.

" Upon the Song of Songs, six books.

" Upon Ezra and Nehemiah, three books.

" Upon the Book of the blessed Father Tobias, one book of Allegorical Explanation concerning Christ and the church.

" Also Chapters of Lessons upon the Pentateuch of Moses, Joshua, and Judges.

" Upon the Books of Kings and Chronicles.

" Upon the Books of the blessed Father Job.

" Upon the Proverbs, Ecclesiastes, and the Song of Songs.

" Upon the Prophet Isaiah, as also upon Ezra and Nehemiah.

" Four books upon the Gospel of St. Mark.

" Upon the Gospel of St. Luke, six books.

" Of Homilies upon the Gospel, two books.   Upon the Apostle[1] . . . .   I have carefully transcribed and reduced into order all the explanations which I have discovered throughout the treatises of St. Augustine.

" Two books upon the Acts of the Apostles.

" Upon each of the Seven Canonical Epistles, a separate book.

" Three books upon the Apocalypse of St. John.

" Also, Chapters of Lessons upon the whole of the New Testament, excepting the Gospel.

" Also a book of Epistles to different persons ; of which one is concerning the Six Ages of the World ; one concerning the Stations of the Children of Israel ; one upon the Words of Isaiah, ' And they shall be shut up in the prison, and after many days they shall be visited ; ' one concerning the Reason of Leap Year ; one about the Equinox, according to Anatolius.

" Also, of the Histories of the Saints, I have translated into prose, from the metrical work of Paulinus, the book concerning the Life and Passion of St. Felix the Confessor.   The book of the Life and Passion of St. Anastasius, which had been badly translated from the Greek, and still worse corrected by some incompetent person, I have amended, as far as the sense is concerned, to the best of my ability.   I have written the Life of the Holy Father Cuthbert, monk and bishop, first in heroic verse, and then in prose.   The History of the Abbots of this Monastery, in which it is my joy to serve God's goodness, that is to say, Benedict, Ceolfrid, and Huetbert, I have written in two books.

" The Ecclesiastical History of our Island and Nation, in five books.

" A Martyrology concerning the Birth-days of the Saints, in which I have taken care diligently to record all whom I could discover; not only upon what day they overcame the world, but also what kind of death they suffered, and under what judge they were condemned.

---

[1] That is, upon the apostle St. Paul.

" A Book of Hymns, in various kinds of metre, or rhyme.

" A Book of Epigrams, in heroic and elegiac verse.

" Of the Nature of Things, and of Times, of each one book.

" Also, of Times, one larger book.

" A book upon Orthography, alphabetically arranged.

" Also, a book upon the Art of Poetry, to which is appended a smaller treatise concerning Figures or Tropes; that is, concerning the figures and modes of speech employed in the Holy Scriptures."

After having finished these books by his continual application, he died at Jarrow, upon the seventh of the kalends of June [26th May], and there he was buried; but after many years had elapsed, his bones were translated from that place, and were deposited close by the uncorrupted body of the most holy father Cuthbert. In honour of this Beda a porch is consecrated in the northern side of the church of St. Paul, at Jarrow, and reminds the faithful of his venerable name. Even to the present day there is exhibited the place in which he had a little mansion of stone, in which it was his custom, apart from all that could disquiet, to sit, to reflect, to read, to dictate, and to write. He departed upon the very day of the festival of our Lord's Ascension; but we think it is best to narrate the circumstances of his death in the very words of Cuthbert, a disciple of his, who thus addresses a fellow pupil :—

CHAP. XV.—A LETTER CONCERNING THE DEATH OF BEDA, AND OF HIS MODE OF LIFE.

" To [1] Cuthwine, his most dearly beloved fellow-student in Christ, Cuthbert, his fellow-disciple, wishes eternal salvation in the Lord.

" The gift which you forwarded to me I received with the greatest pleasure, and most gladly did I read the letters which you sent in your devotion and learning, in which I found, (what, indeed, I chiefly desired,) that you would cause that holy masses and prayers should be diligently celebrated for our master Beda, that father beloved of God. Wherefore, out of my love for him, it is all the more gratifying for me to comply with your request, and to tell you briefly, but to the best of my ability, how he departed from this world, a subject upon which I understand that you are desirous of obtaining some information.

" He had been labouring under a severe attack of difficulty of breathing, unaccompanied, however, with any pain, for nearly two weeks before the day of our Lord's Resurrection,[2] and in this state he prolonged his life, cheerful, and rejoicing, and ascribing thanks to Almighty God day and night, nay, from hour to hour, until the day of our Lord's Ascension, which happened upon the seventh of the kalends of June [26th May]. He daily read with us, his disciples; he spent the remainder of the day in

---

[1] See the Preface to Beda, § 35.

[2] The festival of Easter fell, in 735, upon 17th April; the commencement of Beda's illness must therefore be referred to about April 3d.

the singing of psalms, and he continued awake during the whole
night in joy and thanksgiving, except when his watchfulness
was interrupted by a moderate slumber. When he awoke he
immediately returned to his usual occupations, and he ceased
not to give thanks to God with outstretched hands. He was a
truly blessed man! He repeated that passage of St. Paul the
apostle, ' It is a fearful thing to fall into the hands of the living
God' [Heb. x. 31], and likewise many other texts of holy Scripture ; and as he was skilled in our mode of versification, he gave
utterance to some lines composed in our tongue, that is, in the
language of the Angles. At this time, being in much compunction
of heart, he composed the following lines in English :—

> ' Before his constrained departure
> No man becometh
> Of thought more prudent
> Than is needful for him
> To consider
> Ere his journey from hence,
> What, to his spirit
> Of good or of evil,
> After his death-day,
> Shall be adjudicated.

" He also chanted anthems according to our use and his own, one
of which is as follows :—' O King of Glory, God of might, Thou
who didst this day ascend in triumph above all heavens, leave us
not orphans, but send to us the promise of the Father, the Spirit
of truth. Halleluiah !' And when he came to the words, ' Leave
us not orphans,' he burst into tears, and wept much, and an hour
afterwards he resumed what he had before commenced : and as we
listened to what he said, we also wept; one while we read, another
while we wept ; nay, rather, our reading was always mingled with
tears. In such joy as this we spent the fifty days until the arrival
of the day which I have already mentioned ; he all the while greatly
rejoicing and giving God thanks for that He had thought him
worthy of such suffering. He frequently recalled to mind and
repeated the text, ' God scourgeth every son whom He receiveth,'
[Heb. xii. 6,] and also many other passages of holy Scripture. He
quoted also that saying of St. Ambrose, ' I have not so lived that
I am ashamed to live longer amongst you ; nor do I fear to die,
because our God is merciful.'

" In addition to the lessons which we received from him, and the
singing of psalms, there were two works which at this time he was
particularly anxious to finish, and both of these were of considerable
importance. He was translating into our tongue the Gospel of St.
John, for the use of the church, and he was busy in making some
selections from the book of the Rotæ of bishop Isidore. ' I am
unwilling,' he said, ' that my scholars should read anything which
is not true, and that they should labour unprofitably in this matter
after my decease.' But when the third day[1] before our Lord's
Ascension had arrived, his breathing became more laborious, and a
trifling swelling appeared in his feet ; but he spent the whole of that
day in teaching and dictating with cheerfulness. Amongst his

[1] Tuesday, 24th May.

other observations he sometimes said, ' Learn quickly, for I know
not how long I may abide, nor how speedily He who created me
may remove me.' It appeared to us that he himself was well
aware of his departure. Then he spent the night wakefully in the
giving of thanks to God.

" When the morning dawned upon the fourth day of the week,[1]
he commanded that we should diligently write that which we had
commenced. Having done this until the third hour, we then
walked in procession with the relics of the saints, as the custom of
that day requires us to do. One of us, however, remained with
him, who said to him, ' Still, dearest master, one chapter remains
undone ; would it be troublesome to you were I to ask a few more
questions ? ' He replied, ' The task is an easy one ; take your
pen, prepare your ink, and write quickly.' And he did so. At
the ninth hour he said to me, ' I have a few things of some value
in my coffer ; some spices, and stoles, and incense. Run quickly
and summon the priests of our monastery to come to me, that I
may distribute amongst them these presents, trifling ones indeed, but
such as God has given to me. The rich ones of this world are
anxious to give gold and silver, and other costly presents ; but I,
with much love and joy, will distribute amongst my brethren what
God has given to me.' He addressed each of them separately,
admonishing them, and entreating them that they should be diligent
in celebrating masses and prayers for him ; and this they readily
promised that they would do.

" All mourned and wept, chiefly for this, that he told them that
they should no longer see his face in this world ; but they rejoiced
when he said, ' It is time that I return to Him who made me, who
created me, and who formed me out of nothing. I have lived a
long life, and the merciful Judge has so provided for me that my
life has been a happy one. The time of my release is at hand, for
I long to depart that I may be with Christ.' And with many
remarks of the same kind he passed the day joyfully until the
evening. Then the boy, whom we have already mentioned, said,
' Dear master, there is still one more sentence which has not been
written out.' He replied, ' Write it quickly.' After a little while
the lad said, ' Now at last it is ended.' Beda answered, ' You
have spoken the truth, for it is finished. Raise up my head in your
hands, for it pleases me much to recline in such a position as that
I may look upon that holy place of mine in which I used to pray,
so that while resting there I may call upon God my Father.' And
so, having been placed upon the pavement of his cell, he repeated, ' Glory be to the Father, and to the Son, and to the Holy
Ghost ;' and when he was naming the name of the Holy Spirit
he breathed out his own spirit, and so departed to the kingdom of
heaven.

" All those who witnessed the death of our blessed father affirm
that they never saw any one depart from this life with so great
devotion and calmness. For, as you have just heard, as long as
the soul was in the body he continued to sing, Glory be to the

[1] Wednesday, 25th May.

Father,' and other spiritual songs; and this he did with out-stretched hands to the living and the true God.   Be assured of this, dearest brother, that I could tell you many other things about him; but want of skill in expression enforces brevity in writing."

_____

CHAP. XVI.[1]—WHEN AND WHERE KING CEOLWULF BECAME A MONK; AND OF THE GIFTS WHICH HE GAVE, AND WHO IT WAS WHO REMOVED HIS BODY TO NORHAM.

IN the third year[2] after Beda had fallen asleep in Christ, king Ceolwulf abandoned his kingdom and the cares of this life; and in voluntary poverty he became a follower of Him who had not where to lay his head, that with Him he might be made rich in glory.   He was succeeded in the kingdom of Northumbria by Eadbert, his uncle's son.   When he entered the monastery of Lindisfarne, he gave to St. Cuthbert his royal treasures and lands, that is to say, Bregesne[3] and Werceworde, with their appurtenances, together with the church which he had built there, and four other vills also, Wude-cestre,[4] Hwitingham, Eadulfingham, and Eagwulfingham.   Having received the tonsure in the said monastery, it was his delight to live a monastic life amongst the monks, and after having been a ruler upon earth to become a soldier for the kingdom of heaven.   And here, after having gloriously finished his course, he died and was buried; but some time afterwards (as we shall have occasion to mention[5] presently) he was translated to Norham by Ecgfrid, bishop of Lindisfarne.   At a much later period his head was removed to Durham, together with other relics of the saints, and was deposited with honour in the church of St. Cuthbert, whom he had always loved.

_____

CHAP. XVII.[6]—HOW ONE OF THE ROYAL FAMILY FLED FOR PROTECTION TO THE SANCTUARY OF ST. CUTHBERT, AND HOW HE WAS REMOVED FROM THENCE; AND HOW BISHOP CYNEWULF WAS CAST INTO PRISON FOR HIM; AND CONCERNING THE DEATH OF ST. BALTHER.

DURING the reign of Eadbert,[7] who (as we have already men-tioned) succeeded Ceolwulf, the bishopric of the church of Lindis-farne was held by Cynewulf for some considerable[8] length of time, but under many annoyances and misfortunes.   One of the royal family, named Offa, in order to escape from the persecutions of his enemies, fled to the body of St. Cuthbert, but having been forcibly dragged away from it, he was wickedly put to death.   Hereupon, king Eadbert highly displeased laid hold upon bishop Cynewulf, and commanded him to be imprisoned in Bebbanburch, and in the meantime the bishopric of Lindisfarne was administered by Friothubert, bishop of Hexham, until the king becoming appeased,

_____

[1] In Twysden's edition, book II. chap. i.   [2] A. D. 737.
[3] Perhaps Brainshaugh, near Warkworth, which was also a gift of Ceolwulf.
[4] Woodchester, Whittingham, Edlingham, and Egglingham, all in Northumber-land.   The church of Durham retains the presentation to some of these churches to the present time.   [5] See chap. xx.
[6] In Twysden's edition, book II. chap. ii.
[7] His reign extended from A. D. 737 to 758.   [8] From A. D. 740 to 780.

released Cynewulf from his confinement, and permitted him to return to his church. On the day before the nones of March [6th March],[1] in the seventeenth year of the episcopate of this bishop, and in the twentieth year of the reign of Eadbert, that man of the Lord, the priest Balthere, who had been living the life of a recluse at Tiningaham, entered upon the path of the holy fathers, and departed to Him who had created him anew, even to the image of his Son.

CHAP. XVIII.[2]—CONCERNING THE FORETHOUGHT AND CONVERSION OF KING EADBERT, ABOUT THE EPISCOPATE OF HIS BROTHER, AND HIS OWN DECEASE.

AT this point I interrupt the progress of my history of the bishops, since it appears fitting that I should make a few brief remarks upon king Eadbert. He was the son of Eata, the uncle of king Ceolwulf, as I have already stated,[3] who when he had mounted the throne gave proof that he was fully competent to fill it, and to retain it with energy and success. When at length he had either reduced to subjection or overcome in battle all who opposed him, not only did all the neighbouring kings of the Angles, Picts, Britons, and Scots keep peace with him, but were happy in showing him marks of deference. So wide did the reputation of his good deeds extend, that they reached even to Pepin the king of the Franks, who, in consequence, entered into a friendly correspondence with him, and sent him many different kinds of royal gifts. In the twenty-first year of his reign, whilst he was flourishing in peace and dignity, beloved and favoured by all, he surrendered his kingdom to his son, named Osulf, and subjected himself to the service of Almighty God as a clerk, notwithstanding that the kings of the Angles had previously urged him with much importunity not to take this step, and were willing even to have resigned to him a part of their kingdoms as an addition to his own, provided he would consent to retain his position in his own realm. But he preferred the service of God to all riches and sovereignty, and in that service he continued for ten years, even to the end of his life,[4] when he was buried at York, in the same porch as his brother Ecgbert, who had died three years before himself.[5] This Ecgbert whilst a child had been placed in the monastery under father Eata, and when he was grown up he went to Rome along with his brother Egred, where he received the rank of the diaconate, and returned home upon the death of his brother. During the reign of Ceolwulf, and at his request, he was confirmed as archbishop of the nation of the Northumbrians, being the first after Paulinus who received the pall from the apostolic see ; and this dignity he occupied for thirty-two years.

---

[1] A.D. 756. See Simeon's History of the Kings, under this date; and the Acta SS. mens. Martii, i. 448.
[2] In Twysden's edition, book II. chap. iii.   [3] See chap. xvi.
[4] He died upon 20th Aug. 768.   [5] That is, upon 19th Nov. 766.

CHAP. XIX.[1]—CONCERNING THE SLAUGHTER OF KING OSULF; AND AS TO THE PERIOD AT WHICH BISHOP CWYNEWULF RESIGNED HIS BISHOPRIC TO HIGBALD, AND DIED; AND HOW AND WHERE KING ELWOLD WAS SLAIN.

IN the year of our Lord's incarnation seven hundred and sixty, (being the twenty-first year of the episcopate of Cynewulf,) Osulf was wickedly slain by his own domestics, after he had reigned a single year; and he was succeeded by Aethelwold Mol. When he had reigned for six years, Alchred, of the family of Ethric, the son of king Ida, succeeded to the throne; and, in the ninth year of his reign, the treachery of his nobility compelled him to exchange his realm for exile, and in his stead Aethelred the son of Aethelwold was forthwith appointed king. He was driven into banishment in the fourth year of his reign, whereupon Aelfwold the son of Osulf obtained the kingdom of the Northumbrians, and held it for ten years. In the third year of his rule (being the year seven hundred and eighty from our Lord's incarnation,) Cynewulf—whom we have already mentioned—being then in the fortieth year of his episcopate, and worn out with old age and labour, delegated his authority in the government of the church, with the consent of the whole congregation, to Higbald, an energetic personage; and being thus liberated from such cares, he spent the following three years in quiet and prayer. He departed to the Lord in the fourth year [2] of his seclusion, whereupon Higbald ascended the episcopal seat, and ruled it for twenty years. In the sixth year of his pontificate, the aforesaid king Aelfwold was miserably murdered by his duke Sicga, at a place near the vill called Scytlescester, and was buried in the church of Hexham. As he had been a man of exceeding devotion and justice, a light sent down from heaven frequently appeared to many persons at the place where he had been slain. He was succeeded by his nephew Osred, the son of the late king Alchred; but at the end of a year he was expelled from the realm, and took refuge in the isle of Eufonia (that is, the Isle of Man); and then Aethelred, having been recalled from his exile, regained the kingdom which he had previously lost.

CHAP. XX.[3]—CONCERNING THE DESTRUCTION OF THE CHURCH OF LINDISFARNE, AND HOW SPEEDILY IT WAS REVENGED; AND ABOUT BISHOPS HIGBALD, EGBERT, AND EGRED, AND THE LANDS WHICH THEY ACQUIRED.

IN the year from the incarnation of our Lord seven hundred and ninety-three, (being the one hundred and seventh year from the death of father Cuthbert, and the eleventh of the pontificate of Higbald, and the fifth of the reign of that most wicked king Aethelred,) the church of Lindisfarne was miserably filled with devastation, blood, and rapine, and all but entirely and thoroughly ruined. But before we speak of this destruction, let us make a few extracts from earlier writers descriptive of this locality. The

---

[1] In Twysden's edition, book II. chap. iv.
[2] The Saxon Chronicle says that he died A.D. 782.
[3] In Twysden's edition, book II. chap. v.

following passage occurs :—"The island of Lindisfarne is eight miles in circumference, in which is a noble monastery, the resting place of the bodies of that excellent bishop Cuthbert, and others, his most worthy successors in the episcopate, of whom it may well be said in the words of the anthem, 'Their bodies are buried in peace, and their names shall live for ever.'[1] It takes its name of Lindisfarne from a stream about two feet broad called the Lindis, which here falls into the sea, and which is not perceptible except at low water." So much, then, as to the island itself. Its approaching destruction, and that of other holy places, was presaged by the appearance of fearful thunders and fiery dragons flying through the sky. Presently after this, and in the same year, a fleet of the pagans arrived in Britain from the north; and rushing hither and thither, and plundering as they went, they slew not only the cattle, but even the priests and deacons, and the choirs of monks and nuns. On the seventh of the ides of June [7th June],[2] they reached the church of Lindisfarne, and there they miserably ravaged and pillaged everything; they trod the holy things under their polluted feet, they dug down the altars, and plundered all the treasures of the church. Some of the brethren they slew, some they carried off with them in chains, the greater number they stripped naked, insulted, and cast out of doors, and some they drowned in the sea. Yet this was not unavenged; for God speedily judged them for the injuries which they had inflicted upon St. Cuthbert. In the following year, when they were plundering the port of king Ecgfrid, that is, Jarrow, and the monastery which is situated at the mouth of the river Don,[3] their leader was put to a cruel death; and shortly afterwards their ships were shattered and destroyed by a furious tempest; some of themselves were drowned in the sea, while such of them as succeeded in reaching the land alive speedily perished by the swords of the inhabitants. Although the church of Lindisfarne had been thus ravaged and despoiled of its ecclesiastical ornaments, the episcopal see still continued therein; and as many of the monks as had succeeded in escaping from the hands of the barbarians still continued for a long time to reside near the body of the blessed Cuthbert.

In the eleventh year from the pillaging of this church died Higbald,[4] upon the eighth of the kalends of June [25th May], after having completed twenty-two years in its episcopate; and in his stead Egbert[5] was elected, and upon the third of the ides of June [11th June] he was consecrated at a place called Bigwell,[6] by archbishop Eanbald, and by bishops Eanbert and Badulf, and others,[7] who met there for his ordination. This occurred in the seventh year of the reign of Eardulf, the son of Earulf, who had

---

[1] Ecclus. xliv. 14.   [2] See Simeon's History of the Kings, A.D. 793.
[3] See p. 453, note [1].
[4] He died 25th May, 802; see Florence. But the Saxon Chronicle ascribes his death to 24th June, 803; on which date, see p. 37, note [4].
[5] If Ecgbert was elected and consecrated upon the same day, 11th June,—which, however, is not here stated by Simeon,—then that event probably took place in A.D. 803, in which year, 11th of June was Trinity Sunday.
[6] Bywell, upon the Tyne.
[7] They were the archbishop of York, and the bishops of Hexham and Whithern.

succeeded to the throne upon the slaughter of king Aethelred. But in the tenth year of his reign he was expelled from the province, and Aelfwold held it for two years ; and afterwards it was under the sway of Eanred, the son of king Eardulf, for thirty-three years. When Ecgbert had spent eighteen years[1] in the episcopate, he died, and was succeeded by Heathured, who spent nine years in the exercise of that authority.   After him, Ecgred was elevated to the dignity of the episcopate, in the twenty-second year of the reign of king Eanred ; he was a man of noble birth, and energetic in his proceedings, taking care to enrich and honour (more than his predecessors had done) the church of St. Cuthbert with donations of goods and property.   For he built a church at Norham, and dedicated it in honour of St. Peter the apostle, and Cuthbert the bishop, and also of Ceolwulf, formerly a king, but afterwards a monk ; and he translated thither the body of that same God-beloved Ceolwulf; he also gave to the holy confessor Cuthbert that same vill and two others of the same name, which he had established at Geddeworde,[2] with their appurtenances ; as also the church and the vill which he had built at the place called Geinforde,[3] and whatever belongs thereto from the river Tees to the Wear.   To these he added, as a further donation to the same confessor, to be held for ever, two other vills, namely, Ileclif and Wigeclif,[4] as also Billingham in Heorternesse,[5] of which he had been the founder.   He died in the sixteenth year[6] of his episcopate, which was the fifth year of the reign of Aethelred, who succeeded his father Eanred ; Eanbert, who was elected as his successor, governed the church for eight years.

In the year of our Lord's incarnation eight hundred and fifty-four (being the fifth year of the rule of Osbert, the successor of Aethelred, who had been put to death), the government of the episcopal chair was undertaken by Eardulf, a man of great merit ; nor did he bestow less pastoral solicitude upon the remoter portions of his diocese than upon the more contiguous district of Lindisfarne. Luel, which is now called Carlisle,[7] was one of these ; not only had it belonged to the jurisdiction of St. Cuthbert, but from the time of king Ecgfrid it had constantly formed a portion of the district over which he exercised episcopal jurisdiction[8] . . . .   None of his predecessors or successors even to the present time, endured such labours in the company of the blessed body of Cuthbert ; for during seven years he accompanied it from place to place, fleeing from the savage attacks of the barbarians, whose swords were always ready to slay them ; and (as we shall have occasion to describe presently) the bishop with unalterable love always kept close by the saint, while on every side monasteries were being burnt down, the country plundered, and the inhabitants slaughtered.

---

[1] For this date, see Hardy's Le Neve, iii. 287.
[2] Jedborough, in Teviotdale.   [3] Gainford, in the county of Durham.
[4] Probably Cliffe and Wyclif, in York, but near the river Wear.
[5] A district in the county of Durham, of which the chief town is Hartlepool.
[6] A.D. 850.
[7] And so it continued until the formation of the diocese of Carlisle by Henry I., April 11th, A.D. 1132. See Hardy's Le Neve, iii. 229.
[8] An erasure equivalent to seventeen lines here occurs in the original MS.

CHAP. XXI.[1]—How THE DANES, FOR THE SECOND TIME, RAVAGED THE CHURCH
OF LINDISFARNE, AND ALL NORTHUMBRIA; AND AS TO THE TIME WHEN, AND
THE CAUSE WHY, BISHOP EARDULF REMOVED THE BODY OF ST. CUTHBERT FROM
THE ISLAND; AND AS TO THE SERVICE WHICH THE CLERKS AFTERWARDS
RENDERED.

AT this period there was a large assembly of the people from all
quarters, that is to say, of the Danes and Frisians, and other pagan
nations, who arrived here in an immense fleet, under their kings
and dukes, Halfdene, Inguar, Hubba, Beicgsecg, Guthrun, Oscytell,
Amund, Sidroc and another duke of the same name, Osbern,
Frana, and Harold. On their arrival in England they took possession of it, and wandered over the whole of it, carrying with them
plunder and slaughter wherever they went. After having subdued
and destroyed nearly the whole of the southern provinces of
England, they next attacked the region of the Northumbrians. In the
year from the incarnation of our Lord eight hundred and sixty-
seven (being the fourteenth of the episcopate of Eardulf, and the
fifth of the reign of Aella, king of the Northumbrians, whom they had
placed upon the throne after they had expelled Osbert), the said
army of the pagans, after having taken York, upon the kalends of
November [1st Nov.], spread themselves over the whole country,
and filled all with blood and grief; they destroyed the churches
and the monasteries far and wide with fire and sword, leaving
nothing remaining save the bare unroofed walls; and so thoroughly
did they do their work, that even our own present generation can
seldom discover in those places any conclusive memorial of their
ancient dignity, sometimes none. Upon this occasion, however,
the barbarians advanced no further north than the mouth of the
river Tyne, but returned from thence to York. Urged by this their
necessity, the people of the Northumbrians collected a great army;
their kings, Osbert and Ella, were reconciled with each other; and
they made the attempt, to the best of their ability, to weaken the
forces of their enemy. Headed by two kings and eight earls, they
assaulted York, upon the twelfth of the kalends of April [21st
March], which they stormed with considerable pertinacity, some
from within, some from without. The enemy were somewhat
alarmed by their sudden arrival, but they speedily offered a firm
resistance, and the conflict was waged on both sides with much
fierceness. It ended, however, in the death of the two kings, who
fell along with the larger portion of their followers; and thus
they were deprived at once of life and kingdom, and so paid the
penalty for the injuries which they had previously inflicted upon the
church of St. Cuthbert: for Osbert had dared with sacrilegious
hand to wrest from that church Wercewurde and Tillemuthe, and
Aella had done the like for Billingham, Ileclif, and Wigeclif, and
Crece.

Upon the death of these two persons, the Danes appointed
Ecgbert as king over such of the Northumbrians as survived, limiting

---

[1] In Twysden's edition, book II. chap. vi.

his jurisdiction to those only who resided upon the north of the river Tyne. Having done this, their army advanced from York upon the kingdom of Mercia; but upon their return a few years afterwards, York once more experienced their accustomed cruelty. Departing from thence in the following year, under the command of Inguar (who was the most cruel of all their dukes), their army invaded East Anglia, and first cruelly tormented and then killed the most holy king Eadmund, along with his bishop Hunbert. In the meantime the Northumbrians had expelled out of the province their king Ecgbert and archbishop Wulfhere; and had appointed as their king a person named Ricsig. Not long after this, Halfdene, the king of the Danes, took with him from Rheoppandune, where he at that time was residing, a very large portion of his army; and entering the Tyne with a considerable fleet, he landed at Tomemuthe, where he meant to spend the winter; purposing in the spring to pillage the whole of the district lying towards the north of that river, which hitherto had enjoyed peace.

Having heard of this arrival, bishop Eardulf, (whom we have already mentioned,) apprehensive that the entire destruction of the church of Lindisfarne and of the whole diocese was at hand, deliberated as to the means of escaping along with his followers; but he was uncertain what he should do with respect to the most holy body of father Cuthbert. For it went against his heart that he should ever be parted from that treasure, whether he were resident in the church or driven from it. Having summoned Eadred, a man of approved sanctity, who was surnamed Lulisc, from the circumstance of having been educated in the monastery founded a long time previously by Cuthbert himself in Luel, of which he had now become the abbot,—they deliberated what course it would be most expedient for them to pursue; and, whilst they were so occupied, they bethought themselves of the last words bequeathed to them by the father Cuthbert as he was departing from this life, and so they resolved to abandon the place rather than to yield themselves up as a sacrifice to the barbarians. For, amongst his other admonitions, he had in his parental solicitude given them this advice:[1] "If it should happen that you must decide one of these two things, it would be much more pleasing to me that you should take my bones up from the tomb, and remove them from this spot, and should continue to reside wherever God shall provide an abode for you, rather than that you should tamely submit to evil and bow your necks to the yoke of schismatics." These words when they read them seemed to be prophetically uttered by father Cuthbert in anticipation of their present circumstances; and they saw in them a command applicable to themselves. Raising, then, the holy and uncorrupt body of the father, they placed beside it in the same shrine (as we find it mentioned in old books) the relics of the saints; that is to say, the head of Oswald the king and martyr, beloved of God, which had formerly been buried in the cemetery of the same church, and a part of the bones of St. Aidan, for, as we have already remarked, Colman,[2] on his return to Scotland,

---

[1] See this series, i. 595, § 65.   [2] See chap. v.

had taken with him the other portion of them, together with the venerable bones of those revered bishops, the successors of the same father Cuthbert, (that is to say, of Eadbert, Eadfrid, and Aethelwold,) whom we have formerly mentioned. Having collected these relics, they fled before the barbarians, and abandoned that noble pile, the mother church of the nation of the Bernicians, which had been the residence of so many saints. This occurred in the year of our Lord's incarnation eight hundred and seventy-five, being two hundred and forty-one years since the time when king Oswald and bishop Aidan had founded that church, and had placed therein a bishop's see and a congregation of monks; and one hundred and eighty-nine years after the death of father Cuthbert, and in the twenty-second year of the episcopate of Eardulf. This was the eighty-third year since this church had been devastated under bishop Higbald, as we have already mentioned,[1] by the pirates, and all the monks had been put to death, some in one way, some in another, with the exception of the few who had contrived to escape.

Upon the approach of the tempest of which we have been speaking, all the inmates withdrew; but such of their number as had been brought up and educated from their infancy in the clerical habit followed the body of the holy father wherever it was carried; and unceasingly observed the custom of performing the offices of daily and nightly praise, as they had learned from the monks by whom they had been instructed. Hence it was that the whole body of those who succeeded them observed the usage of singing the hours according to the rule of the monks rather than those of the clerks, following herein the tradition of their predecessors, as indeed we ourselves have oftentimes heard them doing; and as even at the present time some of those persons who are descended from them have reported in our presence. Nor, indeed, was there any laxity upon the part of these monks in their devotion and respect towards the body of this father Cuthbert, who was monk as well as bishop, until the days of this same bishop Walcher. The body was unceasingly attended by bishop Eardulf, who, like his predecessors, was also a monk, and by Eadred, monk and abbot, as long as they lived; and, after these persons, the bishops who succeeded, until the period of bishop Walcher (already so frequently mentioned), were accompanied by two or three monks.

Thus, then, no sooner had the bishop abandoned the island and its church, carrying away with him the relics which we have specified, than a fearful storm swept over that place, and indeed over the whole province of the Northumbrians, for it was cruelly ravaged far and wide by the army of the Danes, under the guidance of king Halfdene. Everywhere did he burn down the monasteries and the churches; he slew the servants and the handmaidens of God, after having exposed them to many indignities; and, in one word, fire and sword were carried from the eastern sea to the western. Whence it was that the bishop and they who with him accompanied the holy

---

[1] See chap. xx.

body, nowhere found any place of repose, but going forwards and backwards, hither and thither, they fled from before the face of these cruel barbarians.

___

CHAP. XXII.[1]—WHY IT IS THAT WOMEN MAY NOT ENTER THE CHURCH OF ST. CUTHBERT; AND CONCERNING THE EXCESSES OF THE NUNS WHO FORMERLY RESIDED AT COLDINGHAM.

IT is a well-known fact, that into scarce one of the churches which the blessed confessor illustrated with the presence of his body,—either at an earlier period or at the present time, either during the time of his flight or after, even to this present day,—has permission to enter been granted to a woman.   How this custom originated, we will now show, interrupting hereby for a little space the sequence of our narrative.

During the period of his episcopate, the monastery of Colding-ham[2] was consumed by a fire, which, though happening accidentally, yet was admitted by all who were acquainted with the circumstances to have had its foundation in the wickedness of the inmates.   In this place resided congregations of monks as well as nuns, which, however, were separated from each other, and resided in distinct dwellings; but they grew lax, and receded from their primitive discipline, and, by their improper familiarity with each other, afforded to the enemy an opportunity of attacking them.   For they changed into resorts for feasting, drinking, conversation, and other improprieties, those very residences which had been erected as places to be dedicated to prayer and study.   The virgins also, who had been dedicated to God, despising the sanctity of their profession, devoted themselves to the sewing of robes of the finest workmanship, in which they either adorned themselves like brides, thereby endangering their own estate of life and profession, or they gave them to men who were strangers, for the purpose of thereby securing their friendship.   It was no wonder, then, that a heavy punishment from heaven consigned this place and its inhabitants to the devouring flames.   The blow, however, did not overtake them without having been preceded by a warning sent by God's mercy; and by it they were for a short time induced to abandon their evil deeds, and to chastise themselves.   But, after the death of the religious abbess Ebba, they returned to their former pollutions, or rather they did worse than hitherto; and while they were saying, "Peace, peace," the heavy wrath of God came upon them.   Not long after this, Cuthbert, that man of God, being elevated to the episcopal throne, careful that an example of this sort should no longer provoke the anger of God against themselves or their successors, entirely secluded them from the society of women, apprehensive that the incautious use of that familiarity should endanger the purpose which they had in hand, and their ruin should afford the enemy cause for rejoicing.   Men and women alike assented to the arrangement, by means of which they were mutually excluded from each other's society, not only

___

[1] In Twysden's edition, book II. chap. vii.   [2] See Eccl. Hist. § 335.

for the present, but for all future time; and thus the entry of
a woman into the church became a matter which was entirely forbidden. Wherefore he caused a church to be erected in the island
on which was his episcopal see, and this the inhabitants called
" Grene Cyrice," that is, The green church, because it was situated
upon a green plain; and he directed that the women who wished
to hear masses and the word of God should assemble there, and
that they should never approach the church frequented by himself
and his monks. This custom is so diligently observed, even unto
the present day, that it is unlawful for women to set foot even
within the cemeteries of those churches in which his body obtained
a temporary resting-place, unless, indeed, compelled to do so by
the approach of an enemy or the dread of fire.

CHAP. XXIII.[1]—ABOUT A WOMAN WHO ENTERED THE CHURCH OF ST. CUTHBERT,
AND HOW SPEEDILY PUNISHMENT OVERTOOK HER.

THERE have been women, however, who in their boldness have
ventured to infringe these decrees; but the punishment which has
speedily overtaken them, gave proof of the magnitude of their
crime. One of these, named Sungeova, the wife of the son of
Bevo, who was named Gamel, as she was one night returning home
from an entertainment, was continually complaining to her husband
that there was no clean piece of the road to be found, in consequence of the deep puddles with which it was everywhere studded.
So at last they determined that they would go through the churchyard of this church, (that is, of Durham,) and that they would
afterwards make an atonement for this sin by almsgiving. As they
were going on together, she was seized with some kind of indefinite
horror, and cried out that she was gradually losing her senses. Her
husband chid her, and urged her to come on, and not to be afraid;
but as soon as she set foot outside the hedge which surrounds the
cemetery of the church, she immediately fell down; and being
carried home, she that very night ended her life.

CHAP. XXIV.[2]—ABOUT ANOTHER WOMAN WHO RAN THROUGH THE CEMETERY, AND
HOW SHE DIED BY HER OWN HAND.

HERE follows another narrative of the same kind. A certain
rich man—who afterwards resided amongst us in this church,
wearing the dress of a monk,—had a wife; and she, having heard
many persons talk of the beauty of the ornaments of the church,
was inflamed, woman-like, with the desire of seeing these novel-
ties. Unable to bridle her impetuous desires, for the power of her
husband had elevated her above her neighbours, she walked through
the cemetery of the church. But she did not go unpunished; for
presently she was deprived of her reason,—she bit out her own

[1] In Twysden's edition, book II. chap. viii.
[2] In Twysden's edition, book II. chap. ix.

tongue; and in her madness she ended her life by cutting her throat with her own hand. For, as it was no easy matter to keep her at home, she wandered from place to place; and one day she was found lying dead under a tree, her throat all bloody, and holding in her hand the knife with which she had committed suicide.

Many other instances might easily be added to these, showing how the audacity of women was punished from heaven; but let these suffice, since we must proceed to other matters.

CHAP. XXV.[1]—CONCERNING THE RAVAGES OF THE DANES; AND ABOUT THE SEVEN BEARERS OF ST. CUTHBERT; AND OF THE VISION OF KING ELFRED.

AFTER this episode, we may now return to the series of our narrative, resuming it at the point at which it was interrupted.

Whilst these pagans were for many years occupying the province of Northumbria, and had settled down in it, its Christian inhabitants, with their children and wives, accompanied the sacred body of St. Cuthbert, esteeming the preservation of that single body an equivalent for the loss of all else,—country, houses, property,—so long as they were permitted to retain it with them. They wandered throughout the whole of the districts of Northumbria, having no settled dwelling-place; and they were like sheep fleeing from before the wolves, placing their entire dependence upon the guidance and protection of their shepherd. Yet it was not permitted to every one indiscriminately to touch the shrine in which the sacred body was deposited; no, not even the vehicle upon which it was carried. Observing the reverence due to such sanctity, out of the whole number seven were specially selected for this purpose; so that, if any matter should require care or repair, no one but these persons should presume to lay their hands upon it. Hence each of them received a surname derived from the nature of the office to which they were collectively appointed.

In the meantime, Aelfred, the king of the West Saxons, unable any longer to bear up against the overpowering forces of the enemy, lay in hiding for nearly three years within the marshes of Glastonbury. It is unnecessary here to repeat—for it is fully recorded elsewhere—how St. Cuthbert appeared to him in a manifest vision, and how, by the assistance of his merits, the king defeated his enemies, and regained possession of his kingdom. Yet this much may be briefly recorded, that, among other of his admonitions and promises, he gave him the assurance that he and his sons should possess the kingdom of Britain. His words were these: " I especially exhort you to observe mercy and justice, and always to teach your sons to regard the same above everything besides; since, by God's gift, through my intercession, the rule of the whole of Britain shall be placed at your disposal. If you are faithful to God and to me, I shall become to you an impenetrable shield, by means of which you shall be enabled to crush all the power of your

---

[1] In Twysden's edition, book II. chap. x.

enemies." So, then, on the morrow, as the saint had promised, nearly five hundred of the king's best friends came to him, about the hour of noon, well armed; seven days after which, the army of the Angles assembled at Assandune, where Aelfred gained the victory over his enemies, and sent royal gifts to St. Cuthbert, by his son Edward. This Aelfred, and his sons after him, being faithful to God and to this holy confessor, performed his directions, and experienced the accomplishment of his promises, in the extension of their kingdom beyond the limits to which it had reached in the times of their ancestors. This was chiefly perceptible in the case of Aethelstan, the grandson of this Aelfred, who was the first of all the kings of the Angles who reduced all his enemies, and obtained the sway of the whole of Britain. How great was the munificence of this individual towards St. Cuthbert and his church, we shall mention in its own proper place hereafter.[1]

CHAP. XXVI.[2]—How THE BODY OF ST. CUTHBERT, WHEN IT WAS ABOUT TO BE CARRIED INTO IRELAND, WAS BROUGHT BACK AGAIN BY REASON OF A TEMPEST.

LET us now return to our former subject. Bishop Eardulf and abbot Eadred, after having wandered over nearly the whole of the province, with the treasure of the holy body, were at last worn out with the fatigue of their daily labour, and began to discuss the expediency of terminating their exertions, and providing a safe refuge for the holy body, by transporting it to Ireland, the more especially as now there appeared scarce the shadow of a hope that they would be able to continue in this country. Summoning, therefore, all those persons who were of approved wisdom and mature age, they opened to them their secret intentions. The project met with their approbation, and they said: "We are clearly admonished to seek for a place of rest in a foreign land; for unless this were the will of God and his saint, doubtless there would long since have been provided for his holy one a place worthy his abode and one convenient for our residence." So then they all of them, bishop, abbot and people, assembled at the mouth of the river which is called Derwent. A ship was there prepared for their transit, in which was placed the venerable body of the father; the bishop and the abbot, and the few to whom their resolution had been made known, embarked, while all the others were kept in ignorance of their intentions. There is no need for many words. They bade farewell to their friends who were standing on the shore, —they hoisted the sails so as to catch the prosperous gale, and the ship speeds on her onward course towards Ireland. How can I describe the grief of those who were left behind at this time? "Miserable men that we are," said they; "why have we fallen upon such days of sorrow? Thou, our father and patron, art like one carried away captive into exile: we, like miserable and imprisoned sheep, are consigned to the teeth of ravening wolves." They had no time to say more; for the winds changed, and the angry waves rose up; the sea, which till then had been calm, became tempestuous; and the vessel, now unmanageable, was tossed hither and thither by the stormy billows. They who were on board became like dead men. Three waves of astounding size struck the vessel, and filled it nearly half full with water; and by a terrible miracle, unknown even amongst the plagues of Egypt, the water was immediately changed into blood. During this tempest the ship heeled over on one side, and the copy of the gospels, adorned with gold figures, fell overboard, and sank to the bottom of the sea.[1] After they had somewhat recovered their senses, and remembered who they were and where they were, they fell upon their knees, and, prostrating themselves at the feet of the holy body, they ask pardon for their foolish enterprise. They put the helm about, and steered the vessel back to the shore and their companions, whom they reached without difficulty; for they were speedily carried thither by the wind, which had now become prosperous. Those who had recently wept for grief, now shed tears of joy. The bishop and his companions, stricken with mingled shame and grief, threw themselves upon the ground at their full length, and with tears earnestly besought that their crime might be forgiven.

CHAP. XXVII.[2]—How those Persons who carried the holy Body were worn out with their daily Labour, and what their Names were; and how St. Cuthbert told them where they should find a Horse, a Bridle, and a Cart; and how they recovered the Copy of the Gospels, which had continued uninjured for three days in the Sea.

At this time the people, exhausted by the long continuance of the labour, and constrained by hunger and the want of every necessary, gradually ceased their attendance upon the holy body, and scattered themselves over these deserted localities, in order that, by some means or other, they might preserve their lives. Indeed, they all went away, with the exception of the bishop, the abbot, and a very few others, exclusive of those seven who (as we have already said) were privileged to bestow more close and constant attendance upon the holy body. It has been remarked on a previous occasion,[3] that these persons had been reared and educated by those of the monks who had conveyed the body of the holy confessor from the island of Lindisfarne, and had resolved that as long as they lived they would never abandon it. Four of them, named Hunred, Stitheard, Edmund, and Franco, were of greater repute than the other three; and it is the boast of many persons in the province of the Northumbrians, as well clerks as laymen, that they are descended from one of these families; for they pride themselves upon the faithful service which their ancestors rendered to St. Cuthbert. So when the others dropped off, these persons alone continued with

---

[1] This MS., one of the most precious monuments of Saxon penmanship which have been preserved to our times, is now in the course of publication by the Surtees Society, the Gospel according to St. Matthew having already appeared. See Beda, p. 546, note [1].

[2] In Twysden's edition, book II. chap. xii.   [3] See chap. xxv.

this great treasure; and as all things seemed against them, they underwent many hardships; nor could they devise any plan by which they might extricate themselves, or lighten the pressure of these calamities. "What are we to do?" said they; "where shall we carry the relics of our fathers? Fleeing from the barbarians, we have now for seven years wandered up and down the whole province: now there is left for us no place of escape in the country; and we are forbidden by the punishment which we have already endured from venturing once more to seek rest in a foreign country. In addition to all this, a severe famine compels us to look for support wherever we can hope to find it; but the sword of the Danes, which is everywhere impending over our heads, prevents us from journeying in company with this treasure of ours. And if we abandon it, and make provision for ourselves only, what answer shall we hereafter make to the people, who will doubtless inquire what has become of their pastor and patron? Shall we say that we have lost it by theft or violence? Shall we tell them that it has been removed to a foreign country, or that we have left it in some unfrequented place? We should assuredly die without delay by their hands, and that deservedly; our memory would be held as infamous by all future ages, and we should earn to ourselves the curses of all men."

Whilst they were giving utterance to these complaints in their distress, the wonted assistance of their affectionate patron did not desert them, but he mitigated at once their mental anxieties and their bodily labours, for the Lord is a refuge to the poor, and a helper in the due time of trouble. He appeared in a vision to one of them named Hunred, and commanded them to make search for the book which (as we have mentioned above) had fallen from the vessel into the depths of the sea; telling him that it was possible that, by God's mercy, they might be enabled to recover that which they thought was gone beyond recovery. The loss of this volume had indeed plunged them in the deepest distress. And he proceeded yet further, adding these words:—"Rise up quickly, and let the horse, which you will notice at no great distance from this place, see a bridle which you will find hanging upon a tree; he will then immediately come to you; do you put the bridle upon him, and yoke him to the carriage upon which my body is placed, and thus you will lighten your own labour." Having heard thus much he awoke, and forthwith he recounted the vision which he had seen, and he lost no time in despatching some of his companions to the sea, which was close at hand, that they might search for the lost book. At this time they were in the neighbourhood of Candida Casa, more commonly known by the name of Hwitern [Whitherne]. When these men reached the shore, the sea had receded much further back than usual, and going out three miles or more they discovered the volume of the holy gospels, which had lost none of the external brilliancy of its gems and gold, nor any of the internal beauty of its illuminations, and the fairness of its leaves, but appeared just as if it had never come into any contact whatever with the water. This circumstance refreshed their hearts with much joy, and left them no room to doubt as to the issue of the other points upon which Hunred had been informed. Exactly as the dream had told him, he saw the bridle hanging from the tree, and, looking around, he discovered a bay horse at no great distance, although he was quite unable to divine how it had found its way into that place of solitude. As he had been directed, he held the bridle aloft, and showed it to the horse, which immediately came to him, and permitted itself to be bridled. He led it to his companions, and from this time they all the more joyfully laboured for the body of the father Cuthbert, then present with them, since they had this undoubted evidence that his assistance would never be withdrawn from them in their hour of need. So, putting the horse to the vehicle which carried the shrine in which that heavenly treasure was deposited, they all the more safely followed him wherever he went, since God had provided them with a horse for his conveyance. Moreover, the book which we have mentioned is preserved even to this present day in the church which is privileged to possess the body of this holy father; and, as has already been remarked, it exhibits no trace of having sustained injury from the water. There is no doubt that this is to be ascribed to the merits of St. Cuthbert himself, and of those other individuals who were employed in its production; that is to say, bishop Eadfrid of holy memory, who wrote it with his own hand in the house of the blessed Cuthbert; and his successor the venerable Aethelwold, who directed that it should be adorned with gold and gems; and the holy anchorite Bilfrid, whose skilful hand carried out the wishes of Aethelwold, and executed this beautiful piece of workmanship, for he was a master in the art of the goldsmith. These persons, influenced alike by their affection for this confessor and bishop beloved of God, left in this work a monument to all future ages of their devotion towards him.

CHAP. XXVIII.[1]—How GUTHRED BECAME KING BY THE COMMAND OF ST. CUTH-
BERT, AND CONCERNING THE PRIVILEGES AND GIFTS WHICH HE BESTOWED.

PROVISION of a resting-place being now made for the saint's body, and they who attended upon him being now enabled to rest after their long labour of seven years' duration, God's justice determined that the wicked king Halfdene should at last suffer the punishment which he had caused by his cruelty towards the church of the saint and other holy places. He was attacked at the same time by mental insanity and the severest bodily suffering; the intolerable stench exhaling from which made him an object of abomination towards the whole army. Thus despised and rejected by all persons, he fled away in three ships from the Tyne, and shortly afterwards he and all his followers perished.

On this occurrence the venerable body was removed to the monastery of Crec,[2] which was built within a vill which had formerly been the saint's own property;[3] and having been most kindly

---

[1] In Twysden's edition, book II. chap. xiii.
[2] A.D. 882.   [3] See chap. ix. p. 637.

received there by the abbot named Geve, they spent four months in that place, as if it had been their own. During this time the army, and such of the inhabitants as survived, being without a king, were insecure; whereupon the blessed Cuthbert himself appeared in a vision to abbot Eadred, that man of holy life, whom we have[1] already mentioned, and, watchful over the repose of his own followers, he addressed him in the following words:—" Go to the army of the Danes," said he, " and announce to them that you come as my messenger; and ask to be informed where you can find a lad named Guthred, the son of Hardacnut, whom they sold to a widow. Having found him, and paid the widow the price of his liberty, let him be brought forward before the whole aforesaid army; and my will and pleasure is, that he be elected and appointed king at Oswiesdune, (that is, Oswin's hill,) and let the bracelet be placed upon his right arm."

When the abbot awoke up he narrated the incident to his companions, and he immediately set out upon the execution of his commission. The young man was produced, and both barbarians and natives reverently accepted the directions of St. Cuthbert, by unanimously appointing him (who had so recently been a slave) to be their sovereign. Having thus attained the throne by their united grace and favour, the troublous storms which had arisen were lulled, and tranquillity was restored; and upon this the episcopal see, which had hitherto been established in the island of Lindisfarne, was transferred to Cuncacestre.[2]

After a residence of four months at Crec, the uncorrupted body of the most blessed father having been translated to Cuncacestre, accompanied by those persons who had attended upon him, the episcopal throne was first occupied by Eardulf, that most excellent bishop, who in prosperity and adversity had clung to the saint with unchanged affection. King Guthred contributed liberally to the church, giving honours and presents; and in his devout humility he constantly and faithfully served him who had raised him to the throne from the condition of a slave. Whatever commands the one gave with respect to the liberties and privileges of his church, and for the support of those who ministered therein, the other, like an obedient servant, immediately put into execution.

The saint once more appeared to the abbot in a vision, and spoke thus:—" Tell the king that he must give to me, and to those who minister in my church, the whole of the district lying between the Wear and the Tyne, to be held in perpetuity, that it may be the means of providing them with the necessaries of life, and secure them against want. Moreover, command the king to appoint that my church shall become a safe place of refuge for fugitives, so that any one who flees to my body, for what cause soever, shall have protection there for thirty-seven days; and that the asylum shall not be violated upon any pretence whatever." Not only did king Guthred give heed to the directions which were communicated by this trustworthy messenger, the abbot, but also that powerful king, whom we have already named, Aelfred, did the same, and

<hr>

[1] See chap. xxi. p. 656.   [2] Chester-le-street, in the county of Durham.

they published them to all the people, and decreed that they
should be observed for ever; while the whole army, not only
of the English, but of the Danes also, agreed thereto, and approved of the same. It was determined that such persons as
presumed in any manner to violate the protection which the saint
had thus established, should be fined by a payment of money;
that is to say, that the fine due to the saint for the violation
of his sanctuary, should be equivalent to the fine payable to the
king for the violation of his, amounting at the least to ninety-
six pounds. Moreover—as the land which he had demanded,
situated between the two rivers . . . .[1] was immediately conveyed to him—it was resolved by the assent of the whole people,
that if any one gave land to St. Cuthbert, or if any land was purchased with his money, that from that time no one should presume
to exercise over it any right of service or custom; but that the
church alone should possess in perpetuity unbroken quiet and
liberty therein, together with all the customs; and (to use the
common terms) with sac and socne, and infangentheof. The
universal suffrage condemned by a sentence of anathema those
persons, whoever they might be, who presumed in any manner to
attempt to set aside those laws and statutes, and consigned them
to the perpetual punishment of the flames of hell, unless they made
satisfaction.

After the lapse of some time the nation of the Scots[2] collected a
numerous army, and among their other deeds of cruelty, they
invaded and plundered the monastery of Lindisfarne. Whilst king
Guthred, supported by St. Cuthbert, was about to engage in battle
with them, immediately the earth opened her mouth and swallowed
them all up alive, herein repeating the ancient miracle in the matter
of Dathan and Abiron. How this was done is notorious, as it is
elsewhere[3] recorded.

_____

CHAP. XXIX.[4]—CONCERNING THE DIGNITIES AND PRIVILEGES OF THE CHURCH.

IN the year eight hundred and ninety-four from our Lord's
incarnation king Guthred died, after having reigned no short time
in prosperity, leaving behind for the protection of others the
inviolable privileges of the church of father Cuthbert. Those of
them which related to the security and liberty of that church, and
to the protection of such persons as fled to his sepulchre for safety,
together with such other statutes as had reference to the security of
the church, Guthred bequeathed in trust to the kings, bishops, and
people of succeeding times; and they are preserved until this
present day. No one who has ventured to infringe them, has

[1] Here occurs a hiatus of nearly two lines, which is filled up, in a recent hand,
by the words "Wear and Tyne."
[2] A more detailed account of this miracle may be seen in the History of the
Translations and Miracles of St. Cuthbert, printed by Mabillon in his Acta SS.
Ord. S. Bened. IV. ii. 298, where the incident is said to have occurred at a place
called Nundingedene.
[3] A reference apparently to the authority quoted in the last note.
[4] In Twysden's edition, book II. chap. xiv.

escaped unpunished. Of this number were the Scots, of whom we have already spoken,[1] who disappeared instantaneously, the earth having opened her mouth and swallowed them up quick, because they had violated his sanctuary; and the following pages shall recount how terrible was the vengeance which overtook those persons whose presumption brought on them a similar punishment. Upon the death of Guthred, king Aelfred had the entire disposal of the whole kingdom of the Northumbrians; for after St. Cuthbert appeared to him he appended to his own kingdom, (that is, the realm of Wessex,) the provinces both of the Eastern Angles and the Northumbrians, upon the death of Guthred.

CHAP. XXX.[2]—ABOUT THE CHARGE WHICH KING ELFRED UPON THE DEATH-BED GAVE TO HIS SON EDWARD.

IN the year of our Lord's incarnation eight hundred and ninety-nine, died that same most pious king of the Angles, Elfrid, after having filled the throne for twenty-eight years and a half, and he was succeeded by his son Edward. This latter sovereign was earnestly admonished by his father, that he should always hold St. Cuthbert and his church in the highest reverence and affection, bearing in mind how great were the perils and calamities from which he had delivered Alfred, and had restored him to the throne, and how he had extended his sway beyond the territorial limits which had been under the jurisdiction of his ancestors.

CHAP. XXXI.[3]—CONCERNING BISHOP CUTHEARD, AND HOW EDWARD BECAME POSSESSED OF THE MONARCHY; AND ABOUT ONLAFBALD, HOW HE DIED WITHIN THE PORCH OF THE CHURCH OF ST. CUTHBERT.

IN the same year in which king Elfred died, bishop Eardulf, of whom we have already spoken, departed from this life in a good old age, that he might receive the reward of his labours. This occurred in the nineteenth year after the holy body of the blessed father Cuthbert had been removed to Cunecacestre, and in the forty-sixth year of his episcopate. In his stead Cutheard, one approved before God and men for the sanctity of his life, received the government of the episcopal see. Provident for the future security of those who should hereafter serve God in the presence of the uncorrupt body of the saint, he made ample provision for their wants, and the charter book of the church (which contains a record of the ancient munificence of kings and other religious persons towards St. Cuthbert) manifestly declares how many were the vills which he purchased by the money of the saint, and added to the gifts which had been contributed by the bounty of former sovereigns.

During the period when Edward was the governor of the king-

---

[1] Namely, in the last chapter.
[2] In Twysden's edition, book II. chap. xv.   [3] Id. chap. xvi.

doms, not only of the Western Saxons, but also of the Eastern Angles and the Northumbrians, and whilst the episcopate of the Bernicians was under the rule of Cutheard, a certain pagan king named Reingwald landed on the Northumbrian shores with a large fleet.   Without any delay he broke in upon York, and either killed or drove out of the country the more influential of the inhabitants. He next seized the whole of the land of St. Cuthbert, and divided its vills between two of his leaders, one of whom was named Scula,[1] the other Onlafbal.   The former of them, Scula, obtained possession of the district from Iodene as far as Billingham,[2] and distressed the miserable inhabitants with heavy and intolerable tributes.   Hence it is that even to the present day the men of Yorkshire, whenever they are compelled to pay a royal tribute, always try to lay a portion of the impost upon that district of the land of St. Cuthbert which Scula held, thereby to lighten themselves.   In other words, they hold as lawful the unjust act of a tyrannical pagan, a man who was in arms, not for the rightful king of the English, but for one who was his enemy, a barbarian, and a stranger; but they are still unable to introduce this evil custom, although they make use of strenuous effort to do so, for it is resisted by St. Cuthbert.   Onlafbal[3] took possession of another part of the vills, and showed that he was even more savage and more cruel than his companion ; but this he did to his own destruction, as was clearly proved to all.   After he had inflicted many injuries upon the bishop, the congregation, and the people of St. Cuthbert, and had laid violent hands upon the farms which of right belonged to the bishop, the latter, anxious to win the man over to God, said to him, " Let me entreat you to lay aside your pertinacious harshness of disposition, and to restrain your hands from thus lawlessly laying hold of ecclesiastical property; for you may be well assured that the confessor will not be slack in punishing you severely for the injuries which you are inflicting upon him and his."   The other, puffed up with the spirit of the evil one, replied, " What is the use of threatening me at this time with this dead man ?   Of what worth is any help which this person in whom you trust can give you against me ?   I vow by the power of my gods that from this time forth I shall be a decided enemy to this dead man, and the whole of you."   The bishop and all the brethren fell down upon the ground, and prayed that God and St. Cuthbert would be pleased to render nugatory these proud threats.   The unfortunate being had at this time reached the door ; one foot was even within the threshold, and one had crossed over it, and there he stood fixed as if a nail had been driven through each foot ; unable to advance, unable to recede, unable to move in any direction.   After having undergone many tortures, he was compelled to make public confession of the sanctity of the most blessed confessor, and then he gave up his wicked spirit in that same place.   Terrified

---

[1] This individual has apparently left a memorial of himself in the name of School Akley, a village a little to the north-west of Darlington.
[2] Eden and Billingham, in the county of Durham.
[3] The punishment of this person is given with greater detail in the narrative printed by Mabillon.   See p. 665, note [3].

by this example, none of the others dared, upon any pretext whatever, from that time forward to seize any of the lands or other property which lawfully belonged to the church.

CHAP. XXXII,[1]—CONCERNING BISHOP TILRED ; AND ABOUT THE COMMAND WHICH
WAS GIVEN AT THIS TIME TO KING ETHELSTAN BY HIS FATHER, AND WHICH
HAD PREVIOUSLY BEEN GIVEN BY HIS GRANDFATHER.

BISHOP Cutheard having now died[2] during the fifteenth year
of his episcopate, he was succeeded in the government of the church
by Tilred, a man of activity. In the seventh year of his pontificate
king Edward died, and was succeeded in the government of the
kingdom by his son Aethelstan, who conducted its affairs with the
greatest reputation. He was the first of the kings of the whole of
Britain who attained to unlimited dominion, and this was by the
assistance of the blessed Cuthbert, who had obtained it for him
from God. For when he had appeared upon a previous occasion to
his grandfather Elfred, he had promised him thus :—" The rule of
the whole of Britain shall be placed at the disposal of your sons by
my assistance." When Ethelstan's father was at the point of death
he repeated all this to his son ; he told him how many and how
important were the favours which the blessed Cuthbert had bestowed
upon his own father ; how he had commanded him to sally forth
from the hiding-places in which he had been lurking from fear of
the enemy, and to attack them ; how he had immediately collected
for him the whole of the English army ; and how, after they had
defeated the Danes with no great difficulty, he had added to the
kingdom, which he had inherited from his ancestors, the greater
part of Britain, and had promised that thenceforth he would be to
him a ready assistant. And the king added :—" Therefore, my
son, take heed to prove that you are upon every occasion a faithful
and devout follower of a patron so influential, and of so kind a
deliverer ; bearing in mind what he has promised to the sons of
Aelfred, if they follow holiness and justice, and are faithful to himself." Aethelstan gave willing attention to these admonitions of his
kind father ; and when he obtained the kingdom, he carried them
out yet more willingly. None of his predecessors on the throne
loved the church of St. Cuthbert as he did ; none beautified it with
gifts so numerous and so regal. Therefore it was that the glory of
his reign surpassed that of any of the sovereigns who had filled the
throne before him ; for he everywhere overcame the numerous
enemies by whom he was assailed from every quarter ; he either slew
them, or reduced them to subjection, or drove them out of the
limits of Britain. In the first year of his reign, that is, in the year
of our Lord's incarnation nine hundred and nineteen, St. Dunstan
was born, who departed to the Lord in the seventieth year of his
age, during the reign of king Aethelred.

[1] In Twysden's edition, book II. chap. xvii.   [2] A.D. 915.

CHAP. XXXIII.[1]—OF BISHOP WIGRED, AND OF THE GREAT GIFTS WHICH KING
ETHELSTAN GAVE TO ST. CUTHBERT AS HE WAS GOING INTO SCOTLAND.

In the year of our Lord's incarnation nine hundred and twenty-five,[2] Tilred died, after having spent thirteen years and four months in the episcopate; and in his place Wigred was elected and consecrated bishop. In the tenth year of his pontificate, when king Ethelstan was on his road to Scotland with the army of the whole of Britain, he came to the sepulchre of St. Cuthbert, requesting his assistance and soliciting his prayers, and he offered many royal gifts of various kinds as an ornament to his church; and these, which are preserved to the present day within its walls at Durham, remain as a perpetual memorial of his pious devotion towards the church of the holy father Cuthbert. The cartulary which contains a regular enumeration of them, makes proof of their character and magnitude. To these gifts of ornaments he added a further donation of vills, no less than twelve in number, for the support of those persons who served within the church; but as their names are recorded elsewhere, it is unnecessary to recount them in this place. Moreover he gave his sanction to the laws and customs of the saint, which had been enacted by his grandfather king Alfred, and by king Guthred, and he directed that they should be inviolably observed for ever. Having made this offering, he laid the heavy curse of an anathema upon such as might dare to take these away, or in any manner to curtail them; that is to say, that they should be smitten in the day of judgment with the same sentence of condemnation as the traitor Judas. At the king's command the army paid honour to the tomb of the holy confessor by the gift of more than ninety-six pounds' weight of silver. Thus having commended himself and his soldiers to the protection of the holy confessor, he proceeded on his journey, and he laid a solemn charge upon his brother Eadmund, that if any misfortune befel himself in this expedition, his body should be removed to the church of St. Cuthbert, and there be buried. But he put to flight Owin, king of the Cumbrians, and Constantine, king of the Scots, and subdued Scotland with an army by land and sea.

In the fourth year after this, that is to say, in the year nine hundred and thirty-seven of our Lord's nativity, Ethelstan fought at Weardune (which is called by another name Aet-Brunnanwerc, or Brunnanbyrig) against Onlaf the son of Guthred, the late king, who had arrived with a fleet of six hundred and fifteen ships, supported by the auxiliaries of the kings recently spoken of, that is to say, of the Scots and Cumbrians. But trusting in the protection of St. Cuthbert, he slew a countless multitude of these people, and drove those kings out of his realm; earning for his own soldiers a glorious victory. Though he was thus formidable on every side to his enemies, he was peaceful towards his own subjects, and having

---

[1] In Twysden's edition, book II. chap. xviii.
[2] This is ascribed to A.D. 922 in Twysden's text, and in Simeon's History of the Kings to A.D. 923.

passed the remainder of his life in repose, he left the monarchy of the kingdom to his brother Edmund.

In the third year of his reign died Wigred,[1] after having filled the episcopal chair for seventeen years, and he was succeeded by Uhtred. King Edmund also, when he was on his way into Scotland along with his army, visited the shrine of St. Cuthbert, and entreated his assistance; and following herein the example of his late brother Ethelstan, he honoured it with royal gifts, namely, gold and precious vestments, and he confirmed the laws of the saint as they had been when they were at their best estate.

CHAP. XXXIV.[2]—HOW ST. CUTHBERT EXPELLED THE SIMONIACAL BISHOP SEXHELM, AND DROVE HIM OUT OF HIS LAND.

UPON the death of bishop Uhtred, Sexhelm was ordained in his room, but after having resided for only a few months in his church, he fled from it, having been expelled by St. Cuthbert. He had widely departed from the precedent of those who had gone before him, and had been driven by his avarice to oppress the people who belonged to the saint, and those who were serving in his church; whereupon the saint terrified him by a dream, and commanded him to depart with all possible speed. Whilst he lingered, the saint appeared to him on the second night, and having rebuked him more severely, ordered him to leave the place forthwith, threatening him with punishment if he tarried any longer. But not even yet was he obedient, whereupon a third manifestation was made to him, more urgent than any of the former; and he was commanded to hasten his departure at once, and to beware how he carried off with him any of the property of the church. He was also given to understand that if he hesitated, death was impending over him. Upon awaking from his sleep, he was seized with illness, and in order to save his life he hurriedly departed, although labouring under this attack of sickness; but as soon as he reached York in his flight his health was restored to him. His successor in the episcopal see was Aldred.[3]

CHAP. XXXV.[4]—OF THE DEATH OF KING EADMUND, AND OF THE EPISCOPATE OF ELFSIG.

IN the year nine hundred and forty-eight[5] from our Lord's incarnation, king Edmund died, and was succeeded on the throne by his brother Eadred, a man who cultivated piety and justice, and one who lavished kingly gifts upon the church of St. Cuthbert, as his brothers had done before him.

Upon the death of bishop Aldred, he was succeeded[6] in the

---

[1] He died A.D. 944.   [2] In Twysden's edition, book II. chap. xix.
[3] See Florence of Worcester, A.D. 944.
[4] In Twysden's edition, book II. chap. xx.
[5] He died 25th May, A.D. 946. See the Saxon Chronicle, ad an.
[6] See the Chronicle of Melrose, A.D. 968.

government of the church at Cunecacestre by Aelfsig, who was ordained at York by archbishop Oscekill,[1] in the time of king Eadgar, who had succeeded his brother Eadwi in the kingdom. After having spent twenty-two years in his bishopric, Aelfsig died; and in his stead Aldhun, a man of devoted religion, was elected, and consecrated bishop, in the year nine hundred and ninety from the incarnation of our Lord, which was the twelfth year of the reign of king Aethelred, who had obtained possession of the royal sceptre upon the death of his brother Edward, who was miserably murdered by the treachery of his stepmother. This bishop was of a noble family, but much more ennobled by his devotion, which rendered him acceptable to God; and, like all his predecessors, he was a monk in habit and mode of life. Even to this present day the inhabitants of the district celebrate his praises, the account of which they have received from their ancestors.

CHAP. XXXVI.[2]—How ALDUNE CONVEYED THE BODY OF ST. CUTHBERT TO RIPPUN; AND HOW HE AFTERWARDS CAME FROM WERDELAU TO DURHAM; AND OF THE NAMES OF THOSE WHO CARRIED HIM.

In the year nine hundred and ninety-five from our Lord's incarnation, and in the seventeenth year of the reign of king Ethelred, when this same bishop Aldun was now entering upon the sixth year of his episcopate, he was admonished by a revelation from heaven, that, carrying with him the uncorrupt body of the most holy father, he should escape by flight, as speedily as possible, from the irruption about to be made by some pirates who were close at hand. So he took the body with him, and he and all the people who are styled the people of St. Cuthbert conveyed it to Hripum;[3] and this was in the one hundred and thirteenth year after it had been located at Cunecacestre. It is worthy of note that in this their flight not one individual of that great multitude, from the least to the greatest, was afflicted with any infirmity, but they all accomplished their journey without any fatigue or inconvenience whatever. Not only did the men, but even the more delicate of their cattle, and those which had just before been born (for it was during spring time that this occurred) endure the fatigues of the road without difficulty and suffering. But after three or four months, peace being restored, as they were returning with the venerable body to its former resting-place, and had now reached a spot near Durham, called Wurdelau, on the eastern side of the city, the vehicle, on which the shrine containing the holy body was deposited, could not be induced to advance any further. They who attempted to move it were assisted by others, but their efforts, though vigorous, were equally ineffective; nor did the additional attempts of the crowd which now came up produce any result in moving it; for the shrine containing the uncorrupted body continued

---

[1] Or Oskytel, who sat at York from A.D. 956—972.
[2] In Twysden's edition, book III. chap. i.   [3] Ripon, in Yorkshire.

where it was, as firmly fixed as if it were a mountain. This circumstance clearly intimated to all that he refused to be reconducted to his former place of residence; but at the same time they did not know where they should deposit him, for the place on which they were at that time standing, in the middle of a plain, was then uninhabitable. Hereupon the bishop addressed the people, and gave directions that they should solicit an explanation of this sign from heaven by a fast of three days' duration, which should be spent in watching and prayer, in order that they might discover where they should take up their abode along with the holy body of the father. This having been done, a revelation was made to a certain religious person named Eadmer, to the purport that they were required to remove the body to Durham, and there to prepare a resting-place for it. When this revelation was publicly announced, all were comforted thereby, and joyfully returned thanks to Christ; and a very few of their number were now able to raise the saint's shrine, whereas the whole multitude had previously been unable even so much as to move it. And thus with joy and thanksgiving they translated the holy body to Durham, the spot which had been pointed out to them from heaven; and, having made a little church of boughs of trees with all speed, therein they placed the shrine for a time.[1] Of those persons who upon that occasion were with the holy body of the confessor, there was one named Riggulf, whose life extended to two hundred and ten years, forty of which immediately preceding his death he had spent in a monk's dress. He was the nephew of Franco, who (as we have already stated[2]) was one of the seven who had followed the holy body of the father without ceasing. Franco was the father of that Reingwald, from whom the village of Reinington,[3] which he founded, takes its name. Reingwald was the father of Riggulf, who had a son named Ethric, and a daughter of this Ethric became the mother of the priest Alchmund, the father of Elfred, who is alive at the present time. This Franco had a companion named Hunred, of whom we have already spoken;[4] and Eadulf the son of Hunred became the father of Eadred, of whom it is reported that for the last six years of his life he could not speak when outside the church, while as long as he was within its walls there was no one who could be more prompt or more skilful than himself in chanting and in singing. There were some who thought that this inability arose to prevent that tongue, which was so studiously exercised in prayers and psalmody, from becoming polluted by idle or harmful conversation. This Eadred had a son named Collan, and he a son who was called Eadred, and Eadred became the father of another Collan, whose sister was the mother of Eilaf, and of the priests Hemming and Wulfkill, who are alive at the present day. What we have said about these persons is sufficient for our present purposes; we will now resume the thread of our narrative.

---

[1] Hence probably the name of the church of St. Mary-le-Bow.
[2] See chap. xxvii. p. 661.   [3] Rainton, near Durham.
[4] See chap. xxvii.

CHAP. XXXVII.[1]—How THE PLACE WAS MADE HABITABLE.

WHEN the whole assembly of the people accompanied the holy body of the father Cuthbert into Durham, it was discovered that the place, although naturally strong, was not easily habitable; for the whole space, with the sole exception of a moderate-sized plain in the midst was covered with a very dense wood. This had been kept under cultivation, having been regularly ploughed and sown; and hereon, at a later period, bishop Aldhun erected a tolerably large church of stone, as will appear hereafter. The said bishop, assisted by all the populace, and by Uhtred,[2] earl of the Northumbrians, cut down the whole of the timber, and in a brief space of time made the place habitable. The entire population of the district, which extends from the river Coquet to the Tees, readily and willingly rendered assistance as well to this work as to the erection of the church at a later period; nor did they discontinue their labours until the whole was completed. When the wood had been uprooted, and a residence assigned by lot to each person, the bishop, in the warmth of his love for Christ and St. Cuthbert, commenced to build a fine church upon a large scale, and devoted all his energies to its completion. In the meantime the sacred corpse had been translated from that smaller church, which we have already mentioned,[3] and removed into another which was called the White Church; and there it remained for the three years during which the larger fabric was being built.

CHAP. XXXVIII.[4]—OF A CRIPPLE WHO WAS CURED AT THE SPOT WHERE THE BODY OF THE BLESSED CUTHBERT HAD RESTED.

WHERE the corpse had rested at the first, miracles began to be performed, and sick people to be restored to health. For, some considerable time afterwards, a certain Scottish woman, who had continued in infirm health all her life long, was brought to Durham; and so great was her misery that her condition excited the compassion of the most hard-hearted. Her feet and thighs were twisted backwards and dragged behind her, and she crept on her hands, and in this posture she dragged herself from one place to another. It so happened that she conveyed herself in this miserable plight to the spot already mentioned, where the most holy body had rested for a few days; and here she suddenly began alternately to leap up (for the veins had resumed their natural position) and to fall again to the ground, and her cries disturbed the whole neighbourhood. After a little time the woman stood upon her feet, erect and strong, and she returned thanks to Christ, who had become her Saviour through the intercession of the blessed Cuthbert. When this was noised abroad, the whole city hastened to the church; the bells were rung, the clergy sung the "Te Deum laudamus;" the people

---

[1] In Twysden's edition, book III. chap. ii.   [2] See Dugdale's Baron. i. 3.
[3] In the last chapter.
[4] In Twysden's edition, book III. chap. iii.

joined their voices in celebrating the praises of God and recording the exploits of the illustrious Cuthbert, the friend of the Almighty. She who was cured travelled .through many regions and nations, performing all her journey on foot ; for she went to Rome to pray, and. on her return she passed over into Ireland, everywhere proclaiming the excellence of the holiness of God and of his beloved confessor, as manifested in the miracle wrought upon herself. We have recorded this miracle, as we have frequently heard it narrated by certain religious and venerable priests who were eye-witnesses thereof.

CHAP. XXXIX.[1]—As to the Period at which Bishop Aldun dedicated the Church at Durham, and about the Gifts with which it was endowed by the Nobility.

Now, to return to our previous narration, the venerable bishop Aldhun solemnly dedicated the church upon the day before the nones of September [2] [4th Sept.], in the third year after its foundation ; and to the great joy of all, and to the honour of God, he translated the incorrupted body of the most holy father Cuthbert, and deposited it with due honour in the place which had been prepared for its reception. And so, up to the present time, the episcopal see remains in this place, along with the holy body, although it had originally been founded by king Oswald and bishop Aidan in the island of Lindisfarne. From that period, I mean from the year in which Aidan ascended the bishop's seat in that island, until the year in which Aldhun mounted that in Durham, three hundred and sixty-one years had elapsed, and three hundred and nine from the death of the father Cuthbert.

The whole of the population, no less than the bishop, was exceedingly delighted with the locality in which the providence of God had been pleased to fix the future abode of the body of his servant, and to manifest that such was his pleasure by the miracle and revelation which we have already recorded. This bishop was a personage of uncommon devotion and humility, and beloved by all good men for his words and actions.

At this time there were very many who contributed divers gifts to the benefit of the church, as well as landed possessions for the support of those who there ministered to the holy confessor. One of these, a nobleman called Styr, the son of Ulf, obtained permission from king Ethelred to give Dearnington,[3] with its adjuncts, to St. Cuthbert; and (in the presence of the king, and of Wolstan, archbishop of York, and Aldhun, bishop of Durham, and the other chief men who had assembled with the king at York) this donation was so confirmed, that a sentence of an eternal anathema was pronounced upon the person who should deprive St. Cuthbert of the gift. The individual whom we have mentioned added some other

In Twysden's edition, book III. chap. iv.
[2] Bedford, in his edition of Simeon, refers the dedication of the church to the year 999, but apparently this date is a year too late. In 998 the 4th of September fell upon a Sunday.   [3] That is, Darlington.

lands, which are recorded in writing elsewhere. Besides these lands, Snaculf, the son of Cykell, added a further donation, that is to say, Brydbyrig, Mordun, Socceburg, Grisebi, with sac and socne. There was other landed property, which bishop Aldhun, compelled by the pressure of the times, transferred (for a period) to the earls of the Northumbrians; but nearly all of these were alienated from the church by the violence of their successors in the earldom.[1] Some of them are here specified by name.[2]   Gegenford (which, as we have already stated,[3] was founded and given to St. Cuthbert by bishop Ecgred), Cueorningtun, Sliddenesse, Bereford, Lyrtingtun, Marawuda, Stantun, Stretlea, Cletlinga, Langadun, Mortun, Persebrige, the two Alclits, Copland, Weardsette, Bincestre, Cuthbertestun, Ticcelea, Ediscum, Werdetun, Hunewic, Neowatun, and Helme. All these were once the property of that church, which, while she sought to benefit those who were in necessity, thereby endamaged her own interests.

CHAP. XL.[4]—CONCERNING KING CNUT; AND OF THE PRAYER OF BISHOP ALDUN, AND HIS DEATH.

IN the year of our Lord's incarnation ten hundred and eighteen, while Cnut ruled the kingdom of the Angles, a comet appeared for thirty nights to the people of Northumbria, a terrible presage of the calamity by which that province was about to be desolated. For, shortly afterwards, (that is, after thirty days,) nearly the whole population, from the river Tees to the Tweed, and their borders, were cut off in a conflict in which they were engaged with a countless multitude of Scots at Carrun.[5]   When the bishop heard of the miserable destruction of the people of St. Cuthbert, he was smitten to the heart with deep grief, and he sighed forth these words: " It is my miserable lot to be reserved to see such days as these are!   Have I lived thus long only to be the witness of such a destruction of my people as the present?   The land will never recover its original condition.   O most holy Cuthbert!   O confessor beloved of God! if ever at any time I have done aught which was well-pleasing in your sight, make me now, I entreat you, some return for the same; and let this be my reward, that, since my people have fallen, I may not long survive them." It was not long before he obtained the request for which he had been a petitioner; for a few days afterwards he was seized with sickness, and died,[6] after having held the bishopric for twenty-nine years; of which number, five were passed at Chester, and twenty-four at Durham. Of the church, the building of which he had commenced, he left

---

[1] At this point there is an erasure of twelve lines in the Durham MS., but the passage to the end of the chapter (omitted in Twysden's edition) is supplied from Leland's Collectanea, L. ii. 137.

[2] Nearly all the places can be identified under a trifling change of name in Durham and the northern part of Yorkshire.

[3] See chap. xx. p. 658.

[4] In Twysden's edition, book III. chap. v.

[5] Probably Carham, on the river Tweed. See Camd. Brit. col. 1096.

[6] A. D. 1018.

behind him nothing more than a western tower, and that in an unfinished condition; the completion and dedication of which were reserved for his successor.

CHAP. XLI.[1]—How a Voice issued thrice from the Sepulchre of St. Cuthbert, in consequence of which Eadmund, a Clerk of the same Church, was promoted to the Bishopric and made a Monk.

Upon the death of Aldhun, the church continued for nearly three years without the protection of a bishop. Its inmates, unwilling any longer to endure this lengthened deprivation, summoned a meeting, and deliberated about the choice of a successor from among their own number. Each of them, in succession, felt it to be hard to leave the pleasures of the world,[2] to abandon its allurements, and to cast aside its pleasures,—hard to submit to carry the heavy yoke of holiness. For, according to the canon law, it was the custom that no one should be chosen as bishop of that church save from among its own inmates; nor could any one, unless of honest and religious conversation, lightly venture to ascend the seat of St. Aidan and St. Cuthbert, and those other holy bishops. Whilst they were deliberating on these matters, one of their number, named Eadmund, a priest of good conversation, joined them, and asked them what they were doing, and why they were so sorrowful; and when he understood that they were treating about the election of a bishop, he said to them, sportively, " Why do not you elect me as the bishop?" Knowing him to be a religious and efficient man, they took his jest as if it were earnest; for they all unanimously agreed to elect him. At first, he believed that they were joking with him; but when he discovered that they were speaking in sober truthfulness, he took the matter deeply to heart, and insisted that in no one particular was he fitted for such a dignity. Whilst they were urging him to undertake it, he replied: " I acknowledge that I am wholly unfit for such an office; but I know that nothing is impossible with God; and I pray that his will, and the will of St. Cuthbert, may be accomplished in me." So then, after they had spent three days before the tomb of St. Cuthbert, (as had been the constant custom heretofore,) in earnest prayers and fastings, entreating him that he would declare by some manifest token who it was whom he should wish to be chosen to the bishopric; and while a certain religious priest was celebrating a mass (which had been appointed for this very purpose) near the head of the saint, as he was in the midst of the canon, he heard a voice issuing, as it were, from the very sepulchre of the father, which thrice proclaimed Eadmund as bishop. The priest forthwith thrice knelt suppliantly before the altar, and when at last he stood erect, he still heard the same voice proclaim, three times, Eadmund as bishop. When the mass was ended, he inquired of the deacon who had stood near him at the sacrifice of the altar, whether he

---

[1] In Twysden's edition, book III. chap. vi.
[2] It will be remembered that Simeon is here describing the secular canons.

had heard anything during the secret of the mass. He answered: "Thrice I heard Eadmund proclaimed bishop, but from whom that voice proceeded, I know not." Then the priest related the facts of the case, as they really stood, to the deacon; whilst all were wondering and inquiring why he bent the knee in the canon, contrary to the custom of the church. Then all, offering their praises and thanksgivings to God through St. Cuthbert, laid hold upon Eadmund and constrained him to take upon himself the government of the church.[1] A certain aged priest was in the habit of giving this account of his election, who stated that he had frequently heard the whole history from his grandfather, who was that very deacon who heard the voice whilst he was reading the gospel in the mass.

So then Eadmund was conducted to Cnut with much honour; and the king himself, rejoicing at his election, commanded that he should be ordained with due solemnity. But he declared that nothing would induce him to mount the chair of his predecessors, who were monks, unless he himself were to follow their example, and, like them, assume the monastic dress. Taking upon himself, then, the religious garb, he was honourably consecrated as bishop at Winchester, by Wulstan, archbishop of York; and he was much beloved and honoured by the king. On his return homewards, he paid a visit to the monastery of Burch [Peterborough]; and he obtained by his entreaties from the abbot a certain monk, who was notably skilled in ecclesiastical offices, and in the observance of the regular discipline, whose duty it should be to bear him constant company, and to instruct him in the details of a monastic life. His name was Aegelric, and he afterwards became bishop of this church of Durham.

This Eadmund was a man of noble origin, and honourable alike in person and behaviour; he never gave occasion for any evil surmises during his whole life, and proved himself energetic in the management of the church. Such as were his enemies had occasion to fear him, as indeed had all wicked people; while he was humble and amiable to every good man. He never flattered the powerful from fear, nor did he suffer the possessions of the church to be lost through the violence of any adversary.

CHAP. XLII.[2]—CONCERNING ELFRID THE PRIEST, HOW ILLUSTRIOUS HE WAS IN THE CHURCH OF ST. CUTHBERT; AND OF THE HAIR WHICH HE PUT IN THE FIRE; AND ABOUT THE MANY HOLY RELICS WHICH HE REMOVED TO DURHAM, UPON THE REVELATION OF THE BLESSED CUTHBERT.

UNDER this bishop there flourished in that church a certain presbyter, whose works of piety and religion had earned for him an intimate familiarity with St. Cuthbert; his name was Aelfred, and he survived until the days of bishop Egelwin.[3] He was a man

---

[1] See Florence of Worcester, A.D. 1020.
[2] In Twysden's edition, book III. chap. vii.
[3] That is, between A.D. 1056 and 1071.

devoted in every respect to St. Cuthbert; of much sobriety, full of almsgiving, unceasing in prayers; terrible to the lascivious and impure, but one who was held in respect by the lovers of what is honest and the God-fearing. He was a most faithful keeper of the church; and one whom even bishops were cautious how they offended, when they knew how intimate he was with the holy confessor. For when bishop Egelric, and his successor brother Egelwin, and the monks who were with them, wished (in addition to the property of the church which they had plundered) to carry off the holy relics of the saints also, and to transfer them to their own monasteries, it is notorious that they were restrained from the commission of this act of injustice by their fear of this priest aforesaid. It was his custom to chant the psalter each night; and when that was done, he used to ring the bell for the nocturnal vigils. Moreover, he was most assiduous in instructing the boys in the service of God; and he carefully taught them, day by day, how to sing and read, and how to conduct the ministrations of the church. He had in his possession one of the hairs of the most holy father Cuthbert, which it was his wont frequently to exhibit to those friends who visited him; and whilst they were wondering at the sanctity of the holy man, he made them wonder still more by means of this hair. For he used to fill a censer with glowing coals, and to lay that hair upon them; and although it continued thereon for a long time, it could not be consumed thereby, but it grew white, and glittered like gold in the fire; and after it had remained there for a considerable period, on its removal it recovered, little by little, its former appearance. Not only did many of his disciples witness this miracle, but one of the brethren of this monastery, named Gamel, a man of much simplicity and humility (who is now asleep in the Lord), affirmed that he had very frequently seen the same occurrence.

Now, while this priest aforesaid was leading an honest and religious life, he was commanded by a vision to visit in succession the sites of the ancient monasteries and churches in the province of the Northumbrians; and he raised from the ground the bones of such of the saints as he knew were buried in these places; and he left them above ground, in order that they might be exhibited to the people, and venerated. I allude to the bones of Balther and Bilfrid, the anchorites; of Acca also and Alchmund, the bishops of Hexham; and of king Oswin: as also those of the venerable abbesses Ebba and Aethelgitha. A portion of all these relics he conveyed with him to Durham, and deposited them along with the body of the father Cuthbert. Admonished by a revelation, he went to the monastery of Melrose, whence he translated the bones of St. Boisil (who formerly had been the master of the blessed Cuthbert in that same monastery), and having deposited them in the church of his disciple, he honourably placed them in a second shrine, (similar to that in which they had formerly rested,) near the body of St. Cuthbert. It was his custom, also, annually to visit the monastery of Jarrow, (in which, as he was aware, the doctor Beda had lived, died, and was buried,) upon the approach of the day of his decease, and there to devote himself to prayers and watchings. Upon a certain occasion he went thither as usual; and after having spent some days there within the church, in solitude, praying, and watching, very early in the morning he returned alone to Durham, (a thing which he had never done before,) while his companions were ignorant of his departure, for he seemed like one who did not choose to have any witness of his secret. Although he survived this event many years, he did not trouble himself ever again to visit that said monastery of Jarrow, but he conducted himself like a person who had secured the object of his desires. Being frequently asked by his intimate friends where was the resting-place of the bones of the venerable Beda, his usual answer (given with the promptitude of a man who knew what he is talking about) was to this effect: " No one knows better about this than I do. Dearly beloved, consider this as a thing most firmly and most certainly established, that the same shrine which contains the most holy body of the father Cuthbert, contains also the bones of the teacher and monk Beda. Let no one seek for any portion of his relics outside the covering of this shrine." Having thus spoken, he enjoined his friends to keep the matter quiet, lest the strangers who were resident in that church should plot some treachery; for their most anxious wish was to carry off, if it were possible, the relics of the saints, and chiefly those of Beda. And, therefore, when he deposited the bones of these saints along with the body of St. Cuthbert, as has been already mentioned, he took good care to do this in private. In entire concurrence with this his opinion regarding Beda, is that poem composed in the English language,[1] which, after having treated of the state of this place, and of the relics of the saints which are therein deposited, makes mention of the relics of Beda, along with the others which are there enshrined. It is well known that his bones were those which were discovered, many years subsequently, wrapped up by themselves in a little linen bag, and deposited along with the uncorrupted body of the father Cuthbert.

Many other memorable incidents are told of this same individual, as having been done by him in compliance with a command given to him in a manifest vision vouchsafed to himself specially by St. Cuthbert, or announced to him as about to happen. For the innocence and pious simplicity of the men who lived at that time were very effective with St. Cuthbert; and in consequence he was in the habit of constantly defending them from their enemies, and speedily avenging any injuries which were inflicted upon them.

CHAP. XLIII.[2]—OF THE GIFTS WHICH KING CNUT BESTOWED UPON ST. CUTHBERT.

CNUT, the pious and religious king of the Angles, venerated with exceeding honour the church of St. Cuthbert, that holy bishop and confessor beloved of God; so much so, indeed, that he walked barefoot to that most holy body from as far as the place which is

---

[1] See it printed in the Decem Scriptores, col. 76, and amongst the Addenda at the end of the volume. [C.]
[2] In Twysden's edition, book III. chap. viii.

called Garmundsway,[1] a distance of nearly five miles; and he gave to the saint, and to those who attended upon him, the mansion of Staindrop, with all its appurtenances, namely Knapton, Scotton, Raby, Wacrefield, Evenwood, Acley, Luttrington, Eldon, Ingleton, Tickley, and Middleton. And he gave them upon this understanding, that no persons, save those who served the saint in his church, should interfere with these localities. And should any one do this, or presume to take aught away, or to curtail the donation, the king and bishop Eadmund pronounced them to be excommunicate; and by this excommunication they became the associates of those who, in the day of judgment, shall depart into everlasting flames. In like manner the same king gave to the saint the vill named Brontun.

_____

CHAP. XLIV.[2]—OF THE SIEGE OF DURHAM, AND THE SPEEDY VENGEANCE WHICH OVERTOOK THE KING; AND ABOUT THE SIMONIACAL BISHOP; AND OF BISHOP EGELRIC, WHO TOOK AWAY THE TREASURES OF THE BLESSED CUTHBERT, AND HOW HE WAS PUNISHED.

IN the year of our Lord's incarnation one thousand and thirty-five, upon the death of Cnut, (when his son Harold[3] was in the fifth year of his reign, and bishop Eadmund in the twentieth of his pontificate,) Dunecan, king of the Scots,[4] advanced with a countless multitude of troops, and laid siege to Durham, and made strenuous but ineffective efforts to carry it. For a large proportion of his cavalry was slain by the besieged, and he was put to a disorderly flight, in which he lost all his foot-soldiers, whose heads were collected in the market-place and hung up upon posts. Not long afterwards the same king, upon his return to Scotland, was murdered by his own countrymen.

When bishop Eadmund was now in the twenty-third[5] year of his pontificate, he died at Gloucester, where he was resident with the king; his corpse, however, was conveyed by his followers to Durham, and was there honourably buried. Hereupon Eadred, the second in order after the bishop, made haste to obtain the bishopric of that church, being the first of the order of the clerics. He extracted from the treasures of the church no small sum of money, and purchased the bishopric from king Hardecnut; but God's vengeance did not permit him to exercise the episcopal office; for as he was about to enter the church he was seized with a sudden sickness, and, taking to his bed, he died in the tenth month.

In this year, that is to say, in the year of our Lord's incarnation one thousand and forty-two,[6] the king himself died, and was succeeded on his throne by the most pious Eadward, the son of king Aethelred and Emma. The see of Durham was obtained by that same Aegelric, of whom mention has already[7] been made. Siward, having put to death earl Eadulf, governed the earldom of the whole

_____

[1] Still called Garmundsway.   [2] In Twysden's edition, book III. chap. ix.
[3] Harold Harefoot succeeded his father A.D. 1035.
[4] This expedition occurred A.D. 1040.
[5] Florence of Worcester says (but incorrectly) that his death occurred A.D. 1048. The truer date is 1041, or 1042 at latest.
[6] See Florence of Worcester, ad an.   [7] See chap. xli. p. 677.

province of Northumbria, from the Humber to the Tweed. But in the third year after he had succeeded to the episcopate; Aegelric was expelled from the church by the clerks, because he was a stranger; whereupon he betook himself to earl Siward, and by a bribe secured his favour and aid against these obstinate people. Terrified and awed by the apprehension of his power, they were constrained to be reconciled to the bishop, whether they would or not, and to readmit him into his episcopal see.   The bishop had with him a monk named Egelwin, a brother of his own, who took the management of the whole bishopric under him; along with whom there were some other monks, all of whom joined with the bishop in studying how to plunder the church of her money and ornaments, and to carry them away.   The bishop thought fit to pull down the wooden church at Cunecaceastre, (which we now corruptly call Ceastre,) and to build there another of stone, because the body of the blessed Cuthbert had for some time remained in that place. So when they had dug to some depth, a great treasure was discovered there, which (as it was reported) the sacrist and a few others along with him had hidden a long time previously, in consequence of the tyranny of Sexhelm, of whom we have made mention above.[1]   The bishop laid hands upon the money and transmitted it to the monastery whence he himself had come; it being his firm intention to follow it thither in person, for his plan was to send before him a quantity of gold and silver, and other articles, which he had removed from the church, and then to resign his bishopric, substituting his brother Egelwin in his place.   By these means Egelwin was elevated to the episcopate,[2] in the fifteenth year of the reign of that most pious king Edward, by the assistance and favour of earl Tosti, who had succeeded Siward; and Egelric, after having been bishop for fifteen years, returned to his own monastery; and he employed the money, of which we have already spoken, in constructing through the fenny regions roads of stone and wood,[3] and churches, and many other things.   But afterwards, during the reign of William, he was accused before him of having taken much money from the church of Durham; [and refusing to refund it,[4]] he was conducted to London, and there imprisoned, and he died whilst in the king's custody.

CHAP. XLV.[5]—OF A PRIEST WHO COMMITTED FORNICATION AT NIGHT; AND HOW, ON THE MORROW, AS HE WAS CELEBRATING MASS, HE SAW A PORTION OF THE BODY, ALONG WITH THE BLOOD, TURN BLACK, AND ON TASTING IT, HOW HE FOUND IT TO BE INTENSELY BITTER.

WHILST this man was bishop[6] an unusual incident occurred, showing, by an awful example, how God's certain anger hangs over the ministers of the altar, if they dare to approach that holy mystery without chastity.   For there was a certain priest, named Feoccher, whose dwelling (where he had a church) was at no great distance

[1] See chap. xxxiv. p. 670.   [2] A.D. 1056; see Florence, ad an.
[3] Concerning these roads, see Ingulf, p. 658.
[4] This clause is erased in the Durham MS.
[5] In Twysden's edition, book III. chap. x.   [6] A.D. 1042—1056.

from the city ; but as he had a wife, the life which he led was unworthy of the priestly office.   One day a large assembly, as well of
nobles as of private individuals, met together early in the morning
at this place, there to hold some law pleadings ; before the commencement of which they entreated the priest to celebrate mass
for them.   Having slept with his wife that night, he was afraid to
approach the office of the altar, and refused to do so.   But as they
urged him, once, and again, and even the third time, to celebrate
mass for them, the priest was in a dilemma ; shame urged him on
one side, and apprehension held him back on the other.   If, on the
one hand, he refused, he was afraid of giving cause for suspicion ;
if he consented, he was apprehensive of incurring the judgment of
a just God.   In the end, however, the fear of man was stronger
than the fear of God, and so he celebrated mass.   But at the time
when he ought to have received the holy mysteries, looking into the
chalice he saw that portion of the Lord's Body, which, according to
custom,[1] he had put therein, changed, along with the Blood, into
a most revolting aspect ; and (as he afterwards confessed) that
which he saw rather resembled the colour of pitch than of bread
and wine.   The priest hereupon understanding his crime, began to
grow pale, and to tremble, as if he already felt himself consigned
to the avenging flames.   Moreover, he was in great trouble as to
what course he should adopt for the disposal of that which he perceived within the chalice ; he shuddered at the thought of receiving
it, as if it were his own death ; he would have gladly cast it upon
the earth, but this he was afraid to do, since it was consecrated.
Having come to the conclusion that whatever he did, he could not
escape the judgment of the Almighty, he received it with great
fear and trembling ; but such was its bitterness that nothing could
be more bitter.   No sooner was the mass ended than he mounted
his horse and hurried off to the bishop, and throwing himself at
his feet he related the whole of the circumstances.   Penance was
enjoined him by the bishop, who gave him in command that, if he
would obtain God's favour, it should be his stndy from that time
forward to lead a life of severe chastity.   This he willingly promised
to do, and the promise which he had made he faithfully kept,
spending the residue of his life in chastity and religion.   That
these events occurred as we have narrated them, rests upon the
frequently-repeated authority of the son of this same presbyter, and
two of the bishop's chaplains, who afterwards were inmates of this
church, having assumed the monastic garb ; and their informant
was the presbyter himself.

CHAP. XLVI.[2]—HOW THE WIFE OF EARL TOSTI SENT A DAMSEL INTO THE CHURCH-
YARD OF THE BLESSED CUTHBERT, WHO SHORTLY AFTERWARDS SICKENED AND
DIED ; AND ABOUT THE IMAGES OF SILVER-GILT.

WHEN he had taken possession of the bishopric, Egelwin contributed nothing to the stores of the church ; nay, his study rather

[1] Concerning this rite, see Durant, De Rit. Ecclesiæ Cathol. II. li. §§ 5 and 6.
[2] In Twysden's edition, book III. chap. xi.

was to abstract from it more of its ornaments and possessions than even his brother had done. But, as the issue of events proved, neither did he escape unpunished ;—more of this, however, hereafter.[1]

During the period of his episcopate, the earl Tosti, (of whom we have already[2] made mention,) having the management of the earldom of Northumberland, always held the church of St. Cuthbert in veneration, and adorned it with no scanty gifts, which are preserved therein even to this present time. His wife also, Judith, the daughter of Baldwin earl of Flanders, an honourable and devout woman, exceedingly loved St. Cuthbert, and contributed many ornaments to his church; and promised that she would add yet more, together with landed possessions, if permission were granted her to enter within its walls, and to pray at his sepulchre. Not venturing to do such a thing as this in her own person, she had planned to send one of her waiting-maids before her, concluding that if the girl could do this in safety, she herself, the mistress, who was to follow after her, would incur no danger. When the damsel had been made acquainted with the pleasure of her mistress, she attempted the exploit at a secret opportunity. She was now in the very act of putting her foot within the churchyard when she began to be repelled by the violence of a sudden gust of wind ; her strength failed her; she was attacked with sickness, and had scarce strength to return to the house, where, falling upon her bed, she was racked with severe pains, which ended only with her life. The countess was greatly terrified at this result, and by way of making a humble satisfaction, she and her husband caused to be made an image of the crucifix, (which, as we shall have occasion to remark hereafter,[3] was plundered of its ornamental work by robbers,) and an image of Mary, the holy mother of God, and of St. John the evangelist, and these they clad in gold and silver, and offered them and many other ornaments for the decoration of the church. At this time also occurred that other miracle about Barcwid,[4] of which a more detailed account is given elsewhere ; who, when he was attempting to violate the sanctuary of the saint, was suddenly smitten with vengeance, and died.

CHAP. XLVII.[5]—OF A MAN ROUND WHOSE NECK A SERPENT TWISTED ITSELF AS HE WAS ASLEEP IN A FIELD, AND HOW IT SPRANG OFF AS HE ENTERED WITHIN THE CHURCH OF ST. CUTHBERT, AND HOW HE WAS DELIVERED.

THERE was also another ill-conducted individual, named Osulf, in whose person occurred the incident which we are about to report, as we have frequently heard the same described by many eye-witnesses. One day, on awaking from a sleep which he had been enjoying in the fields, he discovered that a serpent was twisted round his neck ; he seized it with his hand, and dashed it to the ground, but it twined itself round his neck the second time. Once

---

[1] See chap. lii. [2] Namely, in chap. xliv. p. 681. [3] See chap. l. p. 687.
[4] Reference is made to chap. xvii. of the narrative published by Mabillon, Acta SS. ord. S. Bened. IV. ii. 303.
[5] In Twysden's edition, book III. chap. xii.

more did he throw it on the earth, but he was instantaneously
attacked by it exactly in the same manner as before. It mattered
not whether he threw the snake into the fire, or the water, or on
the ground; it always regained its hold round his neck; how, he
knew not.   Sometimes he took a sword and cut it into pieces; but
forthwith the selfsame serpent was twisting round his neck.   And
at first it was a very little one, but it gradually grew larger and
larger; still, however, he experienced no harm from its venom.
But whenever he entered that church, which is rendered illustrious
by the bodily presence of the most holy confessor Cuthbert, at the
very moment when he crossed the threshold, the serpent left him,
nor did it presume to return so long as he continued within the
fabric.   But whenever he went out it immediately twisted itself
closely round his neck.   After he had endured this annoyance for
some considerable period, he at last fell upon a plan for releasing
himself: for three successive days and nights he remained within
the church at prayer, and when he came out he was thenceforth
unmolested by the grasp of the serpent.   So going on a pilgrimage
he was never afterwards seen in this country.

CHAP. XLVIII.[1]—How a Man who stole Money at the Sepulchre, and put
    it in his Mouth, was punished, and restored.

At the same time there was a man who came along with his
master to the solemn feast of the most holy confessor, and when he
noticed the mass of coin which had accumulated upon the sepulchre
by the offerings of the visitors, he determined to plunder it.   So he
drew near, and (for the purpose of deceiving the people who were
standing round) he pretended to kiss the sepulchre, but in doing
this he at the same time carried off four or five pennies in his
mouth.   Immediately the inside of his mouth began to feel as if
on fire, to such a degree that, according to his own confession, he
seemed as if he were carrying a red-hot iron in his mouth.   He
would gladly have spit out the pieces of money, but he could not
so much as even open his lips.   Tortured with these intolerable
agonies, he ran through the church hither and thither like a dumb
man; and he terrified all the people, for they thought he had gone
mad.   At last he broke out of the church, rushing through the
crowd, and dashed from one spot to another without stopping;
giving all to understand by fearful signs and gestures—for he could
not do so by words—the extremity of his sufferings.   At length,
however, he became more tranquil, and hastily returned to the
sepulchre, and kneeling down at full length, from the depths of his
heart he asked for pardon from the saint, and offered all that he
possessed.   Having made this offering he placed it upon the altar,
and kissed it; and as he kissed the altar, the pieces of money fell
out of his mouth upon the sepulchre.   Thus delivered from his
pains, he lost no time in mounting his horse, and rode off at full
speed, nor did he ever again pay a visit to Durham.   Although he

[1] In Twysden's edition, book III. chap. xiii.

was frequently offered considerable gifts by his lord to return thither with him, he could not be induced to do so; nor indeed did he ever venture so near as to set eyes upon the church.

CHAP. XLIX.[1]—OF THE DONATIONS MADE BY EARL COPSI.

NOT only were this said earl[2] and his wife very devout and munificent to the church of St. Cuthbert, but their friends were equally so. One of them, named Copsi, (who had charge of the whole earldom under Tosti,) made a gift in perpetuity of the church of St. Germans in Merscum,[3] which had been dedicated by bishop Egelric, and the vill thereof, and certain other lands hereafter specified, to the service of St. Cuthbert and his sepulchre, and he, along with the bishops and the assembly, excommunicated all who deprived them of any of these donations, and excommunicated them to be condemned along with the devil. In Merscum he gave ten carrucates of land and a-half. In Thornton,[4] two carrucates of land; in Theostcota, ten bovates of land; in Readeclive, half a carrucate of land; in Gisburham, one carrucate of land. In attestation of this gift he also offered a silver cup, the preservation of which in this church keeps alive for ever the recollection of the fact. At a later time this same Copsi was entrusted, by the advice of king William, with the care of the province of the men of Northumberland, that is, of those who reside on the north of the river Tyne. This, however, was only for a short period.

CHAP. L.[5]—CONCERNING KING EDWARD AND W[ILLIAM]; AND ROBERT CUMIN, WHO WAS KILLED AT DURHAM; AND HOW THE TIDE WAS ARRESTED WHEN THE BODY OF THE BLESSED CUTHBERT ARRIVED IN THE ISLAND.

IN the year of our Lord's incarnation one thousand and sixty-six, the most pious king Edward died, upon the nones of January [5th Jan.], in the twenty-fourth year of his reign, in whose stead Harold ascended the throne of the realm, but he held it only for a short time. For adverse circumstances sprang up around him on all sides; and he engaged in battle against the most valiant king of the Norwegians, in the first instance by two of his earls, and when they took to flight he fought with him personally at no great distance from York. Here indeed he gained the victory; but, proceeding from thence, he encountered in battle the most powerful earl of the Normans, who had just before arrived in England with a large army, and there Harold fell, with nearly the whole body of the English. When William had obtained the kingdom of the English, he, for a long time, bore with the rebellious Northumbrians, over whom he appointed a certain Robert, surnamed Cumin, in the third year of his reign. When the Northumbrians heard of

---

[1] In Twysden's edition, book III. chap. xiv.
[2] That is to say, Tosti and his wife Judith, mentioned in chap. xlvii. p. 633.
[3] Moresham, in Yorkshire.
[4] Thornton, also in Yorkshire, as are also Toccotes and Gisborough.
[5] In Twysden's edition, book III. chap. xv.

this man's arrival, they all abandoned their houses, and made immediate preparation for flight; but a sudden snow-storm and a frost of extreme severity supervening, effectually prevented them from putting their intentions into practice. They all, therefore, came to the resolution of either murdering the earl or of themselves dying together. When the bishop met the earl he told him of this plot, and advised him to return. But the other was not permitted to hearken to these words of counsel, for he was one of those persons who paid the wages of their followers by licensing their ravagings and murders; and he had already killed many of the rustics of the church. So the earl entered Durham with seven hundred men, and they treated the householders as if they had been enemies. Very early in the morning, the Northumbrians having collected themselves together, broke in through all the gates, and running through the city, hither and thither, they slew the earl's associates. So great, at the last, was the multitude of the slain, that every street was covered with blood, and filled with dead bodies. But there still survived a considerable number, who defended the door of the house in which the earl was, and securely held it against the inroads of the assailants. They, on their part, endeavoured to throw fire into the house, so as to burn it and its inmates; and the flaming sparks flying upwards caught the western tower, which was in immediate proximity, and it appeared to be on the very verge of destruction. The people knelt down on their knees and besought St. Cuthbert to preserve his church from burning; and immediately a wind arose from the east which drove the flames backwards from the church, and entirely freed it from all danger. The house, however, which had caught fire, continued to blaze; and of those persons who were within it some were burnt, some were slaughtered as soon as they crossed its doors; and thus the earl was put to death along with all of his followers, save one, who escaped wounded. This occurred on the second of the kalends of February [31st Jan.]. Hereupon king William was bitterly incensed, and despatched thither a general with an army to revenge the death of the earl. But when they reached Allerton, and were about to advance towards Durham on the morrow, there arose such a dark mist that people could scarce recognise each other although standing close at hand; nor could they by any means discover the path. Whilst they were astonished at the occurrence, and deliberating with each other what should next be done, one of them announced that the inhabitants had a saint of their own in their chief town, who always protected them in their adversities, and whom no man could at any time injure without incurring his vengeance. Hearing this, they forthwith returned, each man to his own home; but the people for whose destruction the army had been despatched, knew nothing of their enemies until those enemies had retired. And so it came to pass, (by God's mercy through St. Cuthbert,) that they heard of the retreat of their enemies before they were aware of their march.

But in the same year[1] king William came to York with an army and devastated all the circumjacent districts; whereupon bishop Egelwin and the elders, having had a deliberation among themselves, took up the incorrupted body of the most holy father Cuthbert, and commenced a retreat to the church of Lindisfarne. This was in the seventy-fifth year after it had been conveyed to Durham by Aldhun. They spent the first night in the church of St. Paul at Jarrow; the second at Bedlington, and the third in the place called Tughall; upon the fourth day they reached the crossing to the island, accompanied by all the people of the saint. But as they happened to arrive there about evening, at the hour at which it was full tide, the bishop, and the elders, and the women and the children, mourned and lamented with each other at the danger which they should incur from the winter's cold, (for it was a little before Christmas,) which was sharper than usual. "What shall we do?" said they; "we are prevented from crossing over to the island at this time by the full tide; nor is there any place of residence for us in which we can escape this nipping cold." Whilst they were in the midst of these lamentations, the sea suddenly receding at that spot (but at no other), afforded them the means of passing over, whilst at every other point the tide was at the fullest. All of them immediately entered the island; and thus, singing praises to God and to his blessed confessor, did they reach the island dryshod, along with the holy body of its patron. In this affair one circumstance is worthy of especial notice, and it is a matter the truth of which is vouched for by those persons who at this time were carrying the shrine—that the waves of the sea followed hard upon their footsteps as they advanced, in such-wise as neither, on the one hand, to precede them to any distance, nor on the other, to linger far behind them as they hastened onwards. But when Lent was nigh at hand, and tranquillity had been restored, they carried the holy body back to Durham; and the church having been solemnly reconciled, they entered it with lauds upon the eighth of the kalends of April [25th Feb.], and restored the body to its own proper resting-place. They found the image of the crucifix thrown down upon the ground, and entirely stripped of the ornaments with which it had been clothed by earl Tosti and his wife, whom we have already mentioned.[1] And this was the sole ornament which the monks had left behind them in the church, because it was not easily carried with them in their flight, and they hoped at the same time, that out of respect to it the place itself would be treated with the greater reverence. But some of these people, when they arrived, plundered it entirely of all the gold and silver and precious stones which they could find therein, and then departed. The king was very much incensed at this proceeding, and ordered that they should be hunted out and arrested, and then taken to the bishop and the presbyters, in order that they might be punished at their discretion. But they did them no harm, and permitted them to escape uninjured.

Not long after this, whilst the see was under the rule of Walcher,[2] the king already mentioned transmitted a large quantity of gold and

---

[1] In chap. xlvi. p. 683. [2] That is, between 1071 and 1080.

silver, and very many precious gems, for the ornament of the same image; some of these the bishop employed for that purpose, as may be seen to this present day, some of them his poverty compelled him to expend in alleviating his own wants.

CHAP. LI.[1]—OF THE APPARITION OF ST. OSWALD AND THE BLESSED CUTHBERT, AND THE SUDDEN DEATH OF GILLO, AND OF THE PUNISHMENT WHICH FOLLOWED, AS HAD BEEN FORETOLD.

LET us return, however, to our previous history. In the flight already mentioned, when they were retreating towards the island along with the body of the holy father, there was a powerful individual on the other side of the Tyne, whose name was Gillo Michael; but this, which means The servant of Michael, was a misnomer, and a much more fitting name for him would have been, The servant of the devil. This man inflicted many injuries upon the fugitives; he hindered them in their journey; he persecuted them; he plundered them, and did them all the mischief he could. Not, however, without its punishment. For when the body of the saint had been deposited in the island, a certain aged clerk was sent home by the bishop for the purpose of discovering how things were going on at Durham, and what was the condition of the church. When he had made some little progress in the journey he was overtaken by the night, and having laid himself down in the middle of a field he took a short sleep, in which he had a vision which clearly revealed to him the death of the man whom we have mentioned. As we have frequently heard his account of the transaction, we have thought it best to write the matter down in order.

"I was carried," he said, "to Durham, and was standing, as I thought, within the church, when I perceived that two individuals of great authority were placed in front of the altar with their faces towards the east. One of them was of middle age, magnificently clothed in episcopal robes; and his venerable dress and dignified aspect declared him to be a bishop greatly to be reverenced. The other, who stood at his right hand, was clad in a garment of a ruddy colour; his countenance was somewhat long, and his beard very thin; he was tall in stature, and presented the appearance of a very handsome young man. After a short space of time, they withdrew their eyes from the altar and turned them towards the church; and the bishop, indignant, as it seemed, at its desertion, said, 'Woe to thee, Cospatric! woe to thee, Cospatric! thou hast pillaged our church of its possessions, and hast turned it into a solitude!' For it was owing chiefly to the advice of this Cospatric that the fugitives had abandoned the church; and it was he who had carried off with him the larger proportion of its ornaments. Whilst I was anxious to draw near them, and yet did not dare to do so, the younger of the two pointed towards me with his finger, and in a moderately loud voice he called me by my name, and asked me if I knew who that bishop was. When I answered that

---

[1] In Twysden's edition, book III. chap. xvi.

I did not, 'That personage,' said he, 'is your master, the holy bishop Cuthbert.' I immediately fell at his feet, and entreated him to succour his church in her adversity. Presently they both reverently bowed their heads towards the altar, and advanced from it with a slow and measured step ; and when they had reached the door, the younger of the two stepped forward somewhat in advance of the other, while the bishop stood in the doorway itself. He looked behind him, and calling me, (for I lingered somewhat behind,) he said, 'Earnanus, do you know who that young man is?' I replied, 'I do not know, my lord.' He answered, 'That is St. Oswald.' They now advanced together for some distance, towards the southern side of the city, and then halted. The bishop summoned me to him, and I came ; and at his command I looked downwards, and saw a very deep valley filled with the souls of men. Therein this Gillo Michael, whom we have mentioned, was being tormented with fearful torments ; for he was stretched at length in a filthy spot, and was suffering intolerable agonies, being pierced through and through in all directions with a sharp hay-scythe. The wretch was screaming out, and sending forth, without intermission, fearful yells, dire howls, and pitiful groans ; but there was no intermission in the agonies which he endured, nor was the punishment suspended at any time. All the others were enduring the like torments. St. Cuthbert asked me if I could recognise any one there ; and my reply was, that I could distinguish Gillo. 'You are quite correct,' said he; 'that is the very man: death has consigned him to this miserable infliction.' 'My lord,' said I, 'he is not dead, for this very evening he was at supper in his house, whole and hearty, and there is a great feast prepared for him at this moment at such and such a place, at which he is expected to be present.' He made answer, 'But I tell you of a truth he is a dead man at this moment ; and he, and his companions whom you see with him, are compelled to undergo these pains and torments in consequence of having broken my sanctuary, and inflicted injuries upon myself in the persons of my followers.' When he had said this, I awoke, and immediately I mounted my horse, and entreated my companions to push onwards hastily along with me. Whilst they were wonderingly inquiring the cause of this sudden speed, I told them of the death of this Gillo, and how I had been made acquainted with it. They would not believe my story ; and ridiculed me because I gave credence to it. Thus we journeyed onwards the whole night long, and in the morning we turned aside a short way from the high road, and went to the neighbouring church that we might hear mass. I was questioned by the people, as is a customary thing with them, what news I had brought with me. I announced the decease of the man ; but they affirmed that I was mistaken, as they knew that he was in good health the day before. But immediately some of his household arrived, and stated that their master had died that very night. When I diligently inquired as to the time of his decease, which I did before them all, I discovered that he had died in the selfsame hour of the night in which I had recognised him as dead, and consigned to those horrible torments, of which I had been witness through the guidance of St. Cuthbert. When I recounted his intolerable agonies to earl Cospatric, and had added thereto what I had heard the saint say about himself, he trembled with fear, and immediately proceeded barefoot to the island where that holy body was ; and by prayers and gifts he sought forgiveness for his transgressions. Yet this notwithstanding, he never afterwards recovered the honourable position which he had formerly enjoyed ; for having been expelled from the earldom, the remainder of his life was a series of misfortunes and adversity.[1]

Chap. LII.[2]—Of Bishop Egelwin, who took part of the Treasure; how he was brought back again and captured.

The body of the most blessed confessor having been reconveyed to Durham, as we have stated, Egelwin, in the sixteenth year of his episcopate, carried off a portion of the treasures of the church, and went on board ship, intending to leave England. But when he had sailed towards Cologne, the point which he desired to reach, the wind drove him back to Scotland ; and there he spent the winter. Departing from thence, the retainers of the king laid hold upon him when he was in Ely ; and having been conveyed to Abingdon, he was ordered by the king into close imprisonment. Although he was frequently advised to restore to the church the goods which he had carried off, he affirmed with an oath that he had taken nothing whatever. But one day as he was washing his hands before dinner, an armlet slipped down from his arm on to his hand in the presence of all ; and thus the bishop was convicted of manifest perjury. Being thus cast into prison at the king's command, such was his immoderate anxiety that he refused to taste any food, and died of grief and hunger.[3]

Chap. LIII.[4]—Of the Election of Bishop Walcher, who, however, was a Clerk.

Upon the departure of this individual, the church was without episcopal superintendence for an entire year, after which, in the year of our Lord's incarnation one thousand and seventy-two, (which was the seventh year of the reign of king William,) Walcher was chosen by the king himself, and consecrated to the see of the church of St. Cuthbert. He was a native of Lorraine, of noble birth, amply instructed as well in sacred as in secular literature ; he was of venerable old age, and worthy of this high honour no less from the sobriety of his manners than from the purity of his life. With the exception of that simoniacal personage, of whom we made mention[5] some time ago, who died in a few months, he was

---

[1] See Dugd. Monast. i. 5; and Florence of Worcester, A.D. 1074 and 1075.
[2] In Twysden's edition, book III. chap. xvii.
[3] This occurred in 1071.
[4] In Twysden's edition, book III. chap. xviii.
[5] Namely, Bishop Sexhelm, concerning whom, see chap. xxxiv. p. 670.

the first of the clerical order, after Aidan, who became a bishop of that church; but he showed himself to be a truly religious monk by the conversation of a laudable life. Finding clerks within the church, he instructed them to observe the usage of clerics in their daily and nightly offices; for until this time they had been wont to imitate the monastic customs in these matters, as far as they had learned them, by hereditary tradition from their ancestors, who, as has been already stated, had been trained up and educated amongst the monks.

Chap. LIV.[1]—About King William, who desired to investigate whether the Body of the blessed Cuthbert really rested at Durham; and how he was punished and put to flight.

Some time after this, the king of whom we have been speaking came into Durham, along with his army, upon their return from Scotland, and made strict inquiry whether the body of the blessed Cuthbert rested there; and although all exclaimed aloud, and with oaths, that such was the case, yet he would not believe the statement. He determined therefore to bring the matter to an ocular demonstration, for he had in his retinue certain bishops and abbots who, at his command, would settle the question. He had already come to the resolution, that if the holy body were not discovered there, he would order all the chief of the nobility and of the elder people to be beheaded. So while all were in great consternation, and were imploring God's mercy through the merits of St. Cuthbert, the aforesaid bishop having celebrated mass upon the festival of All Saints [1st Nov.], the king, just as he was on the eve of carrying into execution the intention which he had formed in his mind, was suddenly seized with an excessive heat, the intensity of which so oppressed him that he could scarce endure it. He hastened therefore to leave the church, and paying no attention to a magnificent entertainment which had been provided for him, he hurriedly mounted his horse, and did not draw bridle until he had reached the river Tees. Hence it is evident that St. Cuthbert, one of God's great confessors, rests there, and that the king was not permitted by God to injure the people.

Chap. LV.[2]—How King William sent Ralph to levy a Tribute upon the land of St. Cuthbert; and how St. Cuthbert avenged himself by making the man crazy, and how he was restored; and of the Privileges granted by King William.

Not long after this the king despatched thither a man, named Ralph, for the purpose of compelling the saint's people to pay tribute to the king. They did not relish this, nor were they inclined to submit to new customs; and they took care to seek the aid of St. Cuthbert, who was always ready to help them in the hour of their adversity. On the night preceding the day on which the tribute was to be imposed, the blessed Cuthbert stood before this

[1] In Twysden's edition, book III. chap. xix.   [2] Id. book III. chap. xx.

Ralph in a vision; he struck him with the pastoral staff which he held in his hand, and with the authority which became a bishop, and with a threatening countenance, he rebuked him for venturing to come there to afflict his people; adding, that he should not presume to do this unpunished, and that unless he returned immediately, a worse thing would overtake him. When he awoke from his sleep, he found himself unable to arise from his bed, so great was the weakness which held him back. He at once told all what he had seen and heard; and he humbly entreated them to intercede for him with the holy confessor, promising that he would never at any future time take such liberties with the saint's people, if he might escape with his life upon this occasion. Sending, therefore, a pall to his sepulchre, (which gift is preserved to the present day in this church as a memorial of the incident,) he promised that he would become a faithful servant to him and his, if he would condescend for this once to remit the sin and its punishment. However, as his infirmity increased, he caused himself to be carried upon his litter through various parts of the bishopric, confessing his transgression in the presence of all the people, and showing how it had been punished. This man, as long as he continued within the districts belonging to the bishopric, was continually afflicted with a severe disease; but as soon as he departed from them, and had begun to return homewards, he immediately recovered of his infirmity.

St. Cuthbert having exhibited these and other miracles, king William always held the holy confessor and his church in great veneration, and honoured them with royal gifts, and augmented them with landed possessions. For this king restored to the church Billingham, which, as we have already stated,[1] bishop Ecgred had founded, and given to St. Cuthbert, and which had been withdrawn by the violence of wicked men; and gave it, quit and free from all external customary payment, as a perpetual possession, for the salvation of himself and his sons, to provide food for those who ministered to St. Cuthbert in the church. Moreover, he, by his own assent and authority, confirmed the laws and customs of the saint, which had been established by the direction of ancient kings, and commanded that they should be carefully observed by all.

CHAP. LVI.[2]—How ALDWIN OF WINCENCUMB AND TWO BRETHREN OF EOVESHAM CAME INTO NORTHUMBERLAND, AND HOW THEY WERE RECEIVED BY BISHOP WALCHER, AND WHAT FRUIT THEY BORE.

AT this period there was a man named Aldwin, who was a presbyter of the province of the Mercians, and prior of the monastery situated at Wincelcumbe, a monk in dress and conduct, who gave the preference to voluntary poverty and disregard to the world over all temporal honours and riches whatever. He had understood from the History of the Angles that the province of the Northumbrians had formerly been peopled with numerous bands of monks, and many troops of saints, who, while in the flesh, lived

---

[1] See chap. xx. p. 653. [2] In Twysden's edition, book III. chap. xxi.

not after the flesh, but rejoiced in devoting themselves even while
upon earth, to a heavenly conversation.   These places, that is, the
sites of these monasteries, he earnestly desired to visit, although he
well knew that the monasteries themselves were reduced to ruins;
and he wished, in imitation of such persons, to lead a life of
poverty. So he came to the monastery of Eovesham, and explained
his wishes to some of the brethren, two of whom he forthwith
associated with himself in carrying out the object he had in view.
Elfwy, one of these, was a deacon, but he afterwards became a
priest; the other, who could not read, was named Reinfrid.   Their
abbot would not give them permission to depart, except upon
the condition that Aldwin should previously assume the rule over
them, and should undertake the charge of their souls.   So the three
monks set out together upon foot; taking with them one ass only,
which carried the books and priestly vestments which they required
for the celebration of the divine mystery.   Their first place of residence was upon the northern bank of the river Tyne, at a place
named Munecaceastre,[1] which signifies, The city of the monks: a
locality which, although it belongs to the bishopric of Durham, is
nevertheless under the jurisdiction of the earl of Northumbria.
Wherefore, the venerable bishop Walcher sent for them with the
request that they would come to him, and that they would do better
were they to accept a residence under the jurisdiction of the church,
rather than to remain under the secular power.   When they arrived,
he received them with great respect and joy, and returned hearty
thanks to God for that he had been honoured by having men of the
monastic profession take up their abode within this province, and
under his sway.   So he gave them the monastery of the blessed
apostle Paul, which had been erected at Jarrow by its former abbot
Benedict, the unroofed walls of which were alone standing, and
they exhibited scarce any vestige of their ancient dignity.   Upon
those walls they reared a covering formed of unhewn timbers, with
hay upon them, and there they began to celebrate the offices of
divine service.   Beneath the walls they erected a little hovel in
which they slept, and took their food, and thus they sustained, by
the alms of the religious, a life of poverty.   There, for the sake of
Christ, they took up their abode in the midst of cold, and hunger,
and the want of all things; they, who might have had every abundance in the monasteries which they had deserted.   In the meantime many persons were influenced by their example to abandon
the world, to accept from them the monastic garb; and so they
learned to become the soldiers of Christ under the discipline of an
institution according to rule.   A few of these were from Northumberland itself, but the greater proportion were from the southern
parts of England; and they, following the example of Abraham,
leaving their land, and their kindred, and the house of their fathers,
earnestly desired to become possessors of the land of promise, that
is, of the kingdom of heaven.   Aldwin was an instructor to them
in this religious conversation, for he was one who thoroughly despised the world, most humble in dress and disposition, patient in

---

[1] Afterwards called Newcastle.

adversity, modest in prosperity, acute in intellect, provident in counsel, weighty in word and deed, a companion of the lowly, remarkable for the zeal of his justice against the stubborn, always yearning after heavenly things, and as far as he was able endeavouring to influence others in the same direction.

So when the bishop noticed that the number of the servants of God was on the increase day by day, and that the lamp of monastic life, which had been quenched for so many years in these districts, was once more enkindled by their exertions in his time, he gave thanks to God, and rejoiced exceedingly, and extended to them his solicitude as a bishop and his affection as a father. Observing that their desire was to rebuild the church, and to restore the dwellings of the monks which had been destroyed, he gave them the vill of Jarrow, with its appurtenants, namely, Preostun, Munecatun, Heathewurthe, Heabyrn, Wyvestou, and Heortedun, in order that they might complete their works, and live in comfort. Thus Christ the Shepherd gathered these men from various localities into one sheepfold, teaching them how good and pleasant a thing it is for brethren to dwell together in unity.

CHAP. LVII.[1]—OF THE BROTHER WHO WENT ON A PILGRIMAGE TO STRENESHALCH; AND OF THE FOUNDATION OF THE CHURCH OF THE BLESSED MARY AT YORK; AND HOW WALCHER ONCE MORE RECALLED ALDWIN, AND GAVE THEM WIREMUTHE AND SOME OTHER LANDS.

BUT when Aldwine, the servant of Christ, had now brought forth some fruit in this place, as we have described, he had a wish to visit certain other localities, that in them he might accomplish works of the same nature. So, having placed over the brethren a prior chosen by themselves, he departed from that place, leaving behind him Elfwin, the companion of his former pilgrimage, of whom we have already made mention.[2] He was a man who deserved to be had in remembrance for the simplicity and innocence of his life, and for his constancy in prayers and tears. Their third associate—I mean, Reinfrid—went to Streoneshalch, (which is now called Hwitebi,) in which place he received such persons as came to him, and began to frame a habitation for monks; who, after his death, migrating to York, built a monastery in honour of St. Mary the ever-virgin, which at this time is under the efficient administration of abbot Stephen. But as for Aldwin, when he left the monastery of Jarrow, he took with him, as the companion of his journey and enterprise, one Turgot, at that time a cleric as to his dress, but even then a follower of the monastic life in heart and deed. He came to Durham, and was kindly received by the bishop, who, when he knew his intention, despatched him to the monastery of which we have already spoken; in which he, although a cleric, resided amongst the monks, under the superintendence of Aldwin. For he did not venture to assume the monastic dress before he had made proof of himself by a longer and stricter examination.

---

[1] In Twysden's edition, book III. chap. xxii.   [2] In the last chapter, p. 693.

[He it is who, having succeeded his master Aldwin in the office of prior in the church of Durham, retains that dignity, formerly entrusted to him by bishop William, even to the present day.[1]]

Having followed his master when he departed from the monastery, as we have already mentioned, this man was his constant and inseparable companion. They came to Melrose, which had formerly been a monastery, but was at that time a solitude; and, charmed by the seclusion of the spot, they began there to serve Christ. But Malcolm, the king of the Scots, to whom that place belonged, as soon as he was made aware that they had established themselves there, inflicted on them many injuries and persecutions; since they, observing the precept of the gospel, refused to swear fidelity to him.

In the mean season, the venerable bishop Walcher sent frequent letters and messages to them, in which he entreated, advised, and adjured them,—and at length threatened that he and all the clergy and people would excommunicate them in the presence of the most holy body of St. Cuthbert, unless they would return to him, and dwell under the protection of that saint. Dreading that excommunication much more than the anger of the king, who threatened them with death, (for they were quite prepared for death,) they abandoned that spot, and returned to the bishop. He at once assigned to them the monastery of the blessed apostle Peter, in Wearmouth, which had formerly been a noble and august fabric, as it is described by Beda, who had resided in it from his infancy; but at the period of which we are speaking, its original state could scarce be traced, in consequence of the ruinous condition of the buildings. Here they erected some little habitations of wattle-work, and strove to teach all whom they could influence how to enter in with them at the strait gate, and to walk in the narrow path which leadeth to life. There Aldwin conferred the monastic habit upon Turgot; and as he loved him very dearly as a brother in Christ, he instructed him, by his word and example, how to bear Christ's easy yoke. The bishop, embracing them with familiar affection, frequently invited Aldwin to come, that he might have some conversation with him; and sometimes, taking these persons into counsel with him, he very graciously condescended to obey their suggestions. He endowed them with the vill of Wearmouth, to which his successor, named William, added Suthewic, which is immediately contiguous; with the intention that he, and the brethren who were with him, might continue to serve Christ in that spot without any great difficulty. For some persons came thither from even the very remotest parts of England, for the purpose of spending a monastic life along with them; and so they learned how to serve Christ with one heart and one soul. Then they took pains to clear out the church of St. Peter, nothing more than the half-ruined walls of which were at this time standing; and they cut down the trees, and rooted up the thorns and brambles, which had

---

[1] This passage enclosed within brackets, having been removed from the Durham copy (in which there is an erasure of three lines and a half), is here supplied from the Cottonian MS.

taken possession of the whole site. When they had done this, and roofed it with thatch, as it now appears, they had done their best to make it fitting for the performance of divine services.

We may reckon that two hundred and eight years had passed from the time when the pagans had ruined the churches, and destroyed and burnt down the monasteries, in the province of the Northumbrians, until the third year of the pontificate of Walcher, when the monastic mode of life began to revive in that province, upon the arrival of Aldwin. Thus, under the protection of the bishop, the monks led a peaceable and a quiet life; and he, like a most loving father, condescended to cherish them with the greatest affection, frequently visited them personally, and liberally bestowed upon them whatever they required. It was his intention, had he survived longer, to have himself become one of their order, and to have given a firm footing to the monks near the sacred body of St. Cuthbert. With this design, he commenced the foundations of the monastic buildings as they now exist at Durham; but, alas! death anticipated his plans, and he did not carry them into execution; for the accomplishment of this was reserved for his successor, as we shall have occasion to recount in the sequel.

CHAP. LVIII.[1]—OF THE BISHOP'S ACQUISITIONS; AND OF THE SAVAGE PLUNDERING PERPETRATED BY HIS MEN; AND OF THE THINGS WHICH WERE SEEN AND PREDICTED CONCERNING THE BISHOP AND MANY OF HIS FOLLOWERS, BY A PERSON WHO WAS RESTORED TO LIFE AFTER HAVING BEEN DEAD.

THE firmness of this bishop Walcher not only did not permit any damage to occur in regard to the possessions of the church, but, further, he augmented them by obtaining from the king that valuable property called Waltham, along with its noble church, celebrated for its body of canons. He also had the management of the earldom of Northumberland when the king seized upon earl Waltheof. Of a truth, he was a man worthily beloved by all for the honesty of his life and the sobriety and gentleness of his disposition; but yet he displeased the natives by permitting his followers unrestrainedly to do whatever they pleased, nor did he curb them when they even acted wrongfully. And further, his archdeacon [2] swept away from the church many of its ornaments, and much of its money, and distributed them amongst his own friends and relations. And again, his soldiers carried themselves with excessive insolence towards the people, frequently plundered them by force, and they even killed some of the more influential of them. These ill-deeds of theirs the bishop neglected to punish; nor did he restrain them by the authority of his episcopal office, but just as Eli died for the sins of his children, so was this man put to death for the transgressions of his people, and they and he died together upon the same day.

Shortly before his death, there occurred in the province of Northumberland a miracle, which closely resembles one described by Beda, in his History of the Angles,[3] as having happened a

---

[1] In Twysden's edition, book III. chap. xxiii.
[2] His name was Leobwin, or Leofwin. See Hardy's Le Neve, iii. 301.
[3] E. H. V. xii. § 389.

long time previously,—the restoration of a man to life after having
been dead. This man, Eadulf by name, (who resided at no great
distance from Durham, in a vill called Raeveneswurthe,[1]) fell sick,
and he died one Saturday evening, but he returned to life before
the sunrise of the next morning; and, by suddenly sitting up, he
so terrified the people who were watching by the supposed corpse,
that they took to flight. But as they were running away, he called
them back, and said: "Do not be afraid; of a truth I have arisen
from death; sign yourselves and the house with the sign of the
cross." As soon as he had said this, a countless multitude of little
birds rushed through the door from the outside of the house, and
filled the room in which they were sitting; and they flew backwards
and forwards in such a troublesome manner, as almost to dash
themselves in the very faces of the beholders. So the deacon
(whom the priest had despatched thither when he himself had
returned to the church) ran and sprinkled them and the house with
holy water; and immediately all that ghastly multitude of birds
vanished like smoke from before their eyes. The man who had
risen from the dead related several things respecting the joys of the
blessed and the punishment of the damned, which he had seen
when absent from the body. He also stated that he had recognised
several of his former acquaintance, who were rejoicing along with
the blessed ones in flowery abodes; and he announced that for some
others, who were still alive, the eternal torments of hell were in
preparation. One of these was Waltheof, who afterwards was the
originator of the bishop's murder, of whom he spoke thus, when he
was recounting what he had seen respecting him: "Woe to this
man!—woe to him!" said he; "for him there is prepared a
dwelling-place in the midst of the furnace of hell. There is waiting
for him an iron chair, glowing with eternal fire; the crackling
sparks which fly off from it on all sides are thrown out from inex-
tinguishable flames. On each side of it there are standing terrible
attendants—I mean, evil spirits,—holding chains of iron; and ere
long they will place Waltheof on that seat, and bind the miserable
wretch down upon it with fetters, which cannot be broken, of fire
unquenchable." When he had said this, he inquired where were
the bishop, and his archdeacon, and their followers. When he was
told that they were in Durham, he replied: "All of them are
already dead; the bishop is even now dead, and all his retainers,
who were so puffed up with pride, are as though they had never
existed." Those who were sitting around him, well knowing that
the bishop and his friends were safe, thought that, in so speaking,
he was wandering in his mind; but he once more addressed them,
and said; "I am in my sane senses, and you shall have proof that
I am so, by finding the truth of what I tell you. If I die either
before or after the third day next ensuing, be you well assured that
all that you have heard is false; but if I die upon that third day,
then you shall know for a certainty that I have spoken the truth."
So upon that third day he departed; and, not long afterwards, all
that he had beforehand announced really came to pass: for the

---

[1] New Ravensworth, a little to the south-west of Gateshead.

sudden slaughter of the bishop and his retinue established its truth.
And that miserable wretch, (Waltheof, I mean;) for whose reception he had seen so many infernal torments prepared, after the
murder of the good bishop, was himself slain by his wife's brother,
and so passed to the pains of hell.

CHAP. LIX.[1]—How AND WHERE BISHOP WALCHER WAS KILLED AND BURIED, AND
HOW HE WAS AVENGED; AND HOW THE CHURCH OF THE BLESSED CUTHBERT WAS
PLUNDERED.

BUT let us give a connected narrative of the means by which
this accursed murder of the bishop was perpetrated.

A day had been appointed upon which peace and concord should
be established between the two parties—I mean, the bishop's
soldiers, who had inflicted the injuries, and those persons who had
sustained them. The bishop and his retainers assembled at a place
called Gateshead, where all the elders, and a very large concourse
of the people who dwell beyond the Tyne, had met together, having
banded together for an evil purpose. In order to avoid the crowd,
the bishop entered into the little church belonging to the place,
where he summoned the chief men from among the people to meet
him, that they might discuss arrangements for the advantage of
both parties, and for mutual concord. When this had been done,
and whilst the bishop, with a very few of his followers, remained
within the church, all those who had been summoned thither had
gone out of it, as if for the purpose of deliberation. Shortly after
this, the riotous crowd raised a shout, and then all on the sudden
the work of death was begun, without the least regard being paid to
humanity. Some of the bishop's soldiers, entirely unsuspicious of
evil, sitting or reclining apart from each other, were quickly surrounded and killed; others coming up set fire to the church;
others, with drawn swords and brandished spears, stood at the door
in knots, and suffered none to go out alive; for those who were
within, being unable any longer to endure the violence of the
flames, having humbly confessed their sins and received the bishop's
benediction before going out, were immediately put to death while
they were in the act of crossing the threshold. Last of all the
bishop continued, suffering in his heart sorrows more intolerable
than death itself. It was insupportable for him to see his friends
put to death before his eyes, along with his priests and deacons,
and to know that neither would his enemies spare his own life. In
the meantime, he was in a strait between two kinds of death, and
which of them to choose he knew not. On the one side the flames
drove him upon the weapons of the enemy, and the weapons of the
enemy drove him back again into the flames. The longer the delay,
the greater was the misery; whatever hastened the approach of
death seemed to mitigate its bitterness. Unable any longer to
endure the cruel intensity of the raging flames, he recommended
his soul in prayer to God, and going towards the door, he made the
sign of the cross with his fingers; and having covered his eyes and

[1] In Twysden's edition, book III. chap. xxiv.

his head with the pall in which he was at that time robed, he was pierced through, upon the very threshold, alas! alas! with lances; and even his dead body was stricken with numerous wounds, for such was their brutal ferocity, that not even his death could satisfy them. This murder of the bishop, which all must detestate, occurred on the day before the ides of May [14th May], upon the fifth day of the week before Rogation Sunday, after he had held the see for nine years and two months.

When the intelligence of his death reached the brethren of the monastery of Jarrow, they embarked in a little boat and sailed to the spot; and having discovered the corpse of the bishop, (which they had difficulty in recognising, in consequence of the abundance of the wounds by which it had been disfigured,) they placed it, stripped as it was of every covering, within their vessel, and they carried it back with great grief to their monastery: it was conveyed from thence to Durham, where it was interred with a funeral less honourable than became a bishop; for, immediately after this abominable slaughter, his murderers had come thither, and were raging up and down the city, intending to storm the castle, and put to death such of the bishop's retainers as still survived. But they defended themselves manfully, and the assailants, worn out with their ineffectual efforts, and having lost some of their number, raised the siege upon the fourth day, and departed in various directions; and all those persons, whom the murder of the bishop had made objects of detestation both to God and man, either died by some kind of violent death, or, abandoning their homes and property, wandered in exile in foreign lands.

As soon as the intelligence of this transaction was circulated, Odo, bishop of Baieux, who was second only to the king, and many of the chief nobles of the kingdom, came to Durham, with a large body of troops, and, in revenging the bishop's death, they reduced nearly the whole land into a wilderness. The miserable inhabitants who, trusting in their innocence, had remained in their homes, were either beheaded as criminals, or mutilated by the loss of some of their members. False accusations were brought against some of them, in order that they might purchase their safety and their life by money. Moreover, the aforesaid bishop had removed some of the ornaments of the church, one of which was a pastoral staff, of marvellous material and workmanship, for it was made of sapphire; and this, having been deposited in the castle, which was made a garrison for the troops, speedily vanished.

CHAP. LX.[1]—How BISHOP WILLIAM WAS ELECTED AND CONSECRATED; AND OF
HIS GREAT LEARNING, GOODNESS, AND KINDNESS

SIX months and ten days having passed after the murder of bishop Walcher, in the fifteenth year of the reign of William, that king himself elected the abbot of the monastery of the holy martyr Vincent, by name William; and the rule of the bishopric of the church of Durham was entrusted to him upon the fifth of the ides

[1] In Twysden's edition, book IV, chap. i.

of November [9th Nov.]. His ordination did not take place until some little time afterwards, that is to say, until the third of the nones of January [3d Jan. A. D. 1081], being the octaves of St. John the Evangelist, and a Sunday, when it was solemnly performed by Thomas, archbishop of York, in the presence of the king and of all the bishops of England. This William when a youth was one of the clerks of the church of Baieux, and afterwards followed his father into the monastery of St. Carilif, in which he had become an inmate some time previously. Having thus assumed the habit of a monk, he was regarded as one who was especially remarkable above all his fellows for his love and devotion towards the monastic order, and thus he was gradually promoted until he attained the higher offices. For, first, he was prior of the cloister; then he became the chief prior, inferior only to the abbot; then he was elected to be abbot of the monastery which was contiguous to the aforesaid martyr. No long time afterwards, the king of whom we have been speaking, having had frequent experience of his skill in the management of affairs of difficulty, promoted him, by God's direction, to the episcopal office, as has been stated; for he was well adapted to discharge the duties of a bishop—he was exceedingly well versed in sacred and secular learning, a very careful man of business, and so remarkable for good conduct, that he had no equal amongst his contemporaries in this respect. Moreover, such was the keenness of his intellect, that it would have been difficult to have produced the man who could give sounder advice. Along with this grace of wisdom, he was endowed with considerable eloquence; and so tenacious was his memory, that its power excited universal admiration. By his energy and prudence, he had recommended himself, not only to this king of the English and to the king of the French, but also to the apostolic pope. It was gratifying to them to receive a visit from such an individual as he was, and to listen to his discourse, which was no less wise than eloquent. He was moderate in eating and drinking; he always wore mean clothing; he was catholic in his faith, and was chaste in his body; and as he had been admitted to an intimate position near the king, it was his constant care to defend and protect the liberties of monasteries and churches to the utmost of his ability.

CHAP. LXI.[1]—HOW HE EJECTED THE CLERKS FROM THE CHURCH OF ST. CUTHBERT, AND INTRODUCED THE MONKS, WHOM WE HAVE ALREADY MENTIONED, BY THE AUTHORITY OF THE POPE AND THE KING.

WHEN he had obtained the episcopal see of St. Cuthbert by God's favour, he found that the land which belonged to it was nearly desolated, and he noticed that the locality which the presence of his sacred body made illustrious, was in a condition so neglected as to be by no means consistent with his sanctity. He discovered there neither monks of his own order, nor any canons regular. Deeply grieved at this state of things, he earnestly and constantly entreated God and St. Cuthbert that they would aid him

[1] In Twysden's edition, book IV. chap. ii.

first in deliberating how these irregularities were to be amended, and then in carrying his deliberations into execution.   He inquired of the seniors and the more prudent men of the whole bishopric, what was the arrangement which prevailed at the beginning, when St. Cuthbert's episcopal see was in the island of Lindisfarne; and the answer which they made him was, that in life and after death he was attended upon by monks; and this their statement was supported by the history of his life, and the Ecclesiastical History of the Angles.   A considerable period after this, a cruel inroad of the barbarians having devastated not only this spot, as we have already mentioned, but many other places likewise, the illustrious inmates of that monastery all died a cruel death.   Yet not without punishment; for shortly afterwards all these sacrilegious barbarians were fearfully stricken with the just anger of God, and were carried off from this world to the eternal torments of the next.   Having attained this information, his object was to restore the service which had originally been appropriated to that sacred body; and in order that no one should hereafter set aside his arrangements upon the plea that they were his own private acts, he herein asked the advice of king William, and his wife queen Matilda, and Landfranc, archbishop of Canterbury.   Anxious that a design of such utility should obtain general approbation, the king lost no time in despatching him to pope Gregory, to consult with him not only upon this particular piece of business, but upon some other matters, with the management of which he entrusted him.   When the archbishop had recounted to the pope a few out of the many proofs of the sanctity of the blessed father Cuthbert, the project met with his entire approval, that is to say, that he should unite into one establishment the monks whom he had discovered in those two places within his episcopate, Wearmouth and Jarrow; and that they should henceforth form one single congregation around the body of the saint; for the small extent of the diocese did not afford room for these monastic establishments.   Having most devoutly confirmed this by his apostolic authority,[1] he despatched letters by the aforesaid bishop to king William[2] and archbishop Landfranc,[3] in which he bestowed his blessing upon them, and such others as should aid and assist in this laudable enterprise; and hurling his eternal anathema against whosoever should attempt to thwart it, unless they repented and made fitting satisfaction.   When the king heard that the pope had assented in this wise he was no little rejoiced, and he gave his licence for its accomplishment, which was attested by queen Matilda, archbishop Landfranc, and his barons; and besides this, he commanded the bishop to carry it into effect.   In addition to all this, he made a second confirmation of the laws of St. Cuthbert, which he had already ratified and established before his holy body, restoring them to the efficacy which they had at any time before possessed under the most favourable circumstances.

---

[1] Gregory's bull, by which he confirmed the possessions and liberties of the Church of Durham, is printed in the Appendix to the Historiæ Dunelmensis Scriptores Tres, p. vii. ed. 1839.

[2] Id. p. xiv.   [3] Id. p. x.

CHAP. LXII.[1]—CONCERNING THE DAY AND PERIOD AT WHICH THE BISHOP BROUGHT THE MONKS INTO DURHAM, AND HOW HE GAVE THEM HIS BLESSING, AND ASSIGNED TO EACH HIS OWN SEVERAL POST OF DUTY.

In the year of our Lord's incarnation, ten hundred and eighty-three, being the three hundred and ninety-seventh from the death of the father Cuthbert, the eighty-ninth from the translation of his incorrupt body to Durham by bishop Aldhun, the eighteenth of the reign of king William, the tenth from the arrival of Aldwin with his two companions in the province of Northumberland, and the third of the episcopate of bishop William, on Friday, the seventh of the kalends of June,[2] this bishop already mentioned conducted into Durham the monks[3] which he had collected from these two monasteries, that is to say, from the monasteries of the apostles Peter and Paul, at Wearmouth and Jarrow. On the third day afterwards, that is, upon the holy day of Whitsunday,[4] they were introduced into the church of St. Cuthbert, and there the command of the apostolic pope, given by the authority of the blessed Peter the chief of the apostles, was exhibited to the assembled multitudes,[5] who were also informed that it had the approbation of the most excellent king William. When this had been done, the bishop recommended these monks to Mary the most blessed mother of God, and to his most holy patron Cuthbert, and delivered over the church to them, and them to the church. Next, in the midst of the solemnization of the mass,—following the custom of those who profess the monastic usages,—he gave his blessing to those persons who had promised that they would fix their residence in this place, and he bound them by a link which could not be severed to the body of the most holy father Cuthbert. And as for those individuals who had hitherto resided therein, (canons by name, but men who in no one respect followed the canonical rule,) them he commanded henceforth to lead a monastic life along with the monks, if they had any wish to continue their residence within the church. All of them preferred abandoning the church to retaining it upon such a condition, except one of their number, the dean, whose son, a monk, had difficulty in persuading him to follow his own example.[6] . . . .

Three days after the monks had made their profession, the bishop, having summoned a general meeting of their body, apportioned out to such of them as appeared to be the steadiest and most prudent, the various monastic offices or duties, to the discharge of which each of them appeared to be severally the best

---

[1] In Twysden's edition, book IV. chap. iii

[2] Namely, Friday, 26th May, being the festival of St. Augustin of Canterbury.

[3] Here, in the Durham MS. a few words have been erased, which the Cottonian copy supplies by stating that the number of the monks, when they took possession of the new buildings, was twenty-three.

[4] Sunday, 28th May.

[5] This bull, dated the eighth of the ides of January, A.D. 1083, is printed in the collection already cited, p. vii.

[6] Here, in the Durham MS., occurs a hiatus of twenty lines, to supply which Twysden's text affords no assistance. A modern hand has added a few lines, of which the following is a translation:—"It is stated that the prebends of Aukland, Darlington, Norton, and Ekington, and no others, were assigned by the Pope to these canons to provide them with the means of continual support."

adapted.   This he did with discretion and under the fear of God, by the general consent of the whole body.   Beginning in regular succession from the head, that is, the altar, he assigned to one of them, named Leofwin, a prudent man, and one who especially feared God, the care of the church and of the incorrupt body of St. Cuthbert, and him he appointed sacristan.   Then he entrusted Aldwin (of whose prudence, discretion, moderation, and good habits he was well assured) with the care and management, external and internal, of the whole monastery; and he decided that nothing should be done without his advice and superintendence.   Next, he severed with the greatest precision the landed property of the monks from those which belonged to himself, exempting them from all service due to the bishop, and making them free and quit of all customary payments, to supply them with food and raiment; for it was an ancient usage in the church, that they who ministered to God before the body of St. Cuthbert, should have their own lands distinct from those which belonged to the bishop.   Therefore it was that (as we have already stated [1]) king William, upon a previous occasion, had assigned Billingham to them ; and now again, when the monks came to Durham, did he make a second grant [2] to them of that vill and its adjuncts, for the special service of providing food for those persons who ministered in the church to God and St. Cuthbert: and this he did for the salvation of himself and his sons.   The bishop also contributed a small donation of land to the monks ; but he and the king had made joint arrangements for the sufficient provision of the inmates with food and raiment, that there might be no want, no pinching, while they were serving Christ ; and these he was about to convey to them, when the accomplishment of this design was interrupted by the death, first of the king, and then of the bishop.

_____

CHAP. LXIII.[3]—OF THE BODY OF ST. OSWIN; AND OF THE POSSESSION OF THE CHURCH OF TYNEMOUTHE, AND HOW IT WAS TAKEN AWAY BY VIOLENCE.

WHILST the monks were still resident at Jarrow, they had become possessed of the church of St. Oswin, in Tynemuthe, by the donation of the earls of Northumberland;[4] whence it came to pass, that they translated into their own church of St. Paul's the bones of St. Oswin, and kept them there for a long time ; but they were afterwards conveyed to their primitive depository.   And in the time of this said bishop William, the earl of Northumberland named Albrius [5] renewed this donation, and assigned this church with its priest to the church of St. Cuthbert, as a possession to be held in perpetuity.   When it had now continued for fifteen years deserted

_____

[1] See chap. lv. p. 692.
[2] The charter of donation is printed in the Appendix already cited, p. xx.
[3] In Twysden's edition, book IV. chap. iv.
[4] A various reading, furnished by the Cottonian MS., states that the donor was bishop Walcher, while he held the government of the earldom.
[5] This Alberic (a Norman, who was constituted earl by king William, concerning whom see Dugd. Baron. i. 56) was not the donor of Tynemouth, as is shown by existing charters, which prove that it was the gift of earl Waltheof. See the Appendix to the Three Durham Historians already quoted, pp. xviii. xix., and Illustration [D].

and unroofed, the monks restored it, by thatching it over, and kept it in possession for three years. But after Albrius had been succeeded in the earldom by Robert de Mulbrei, the latter drove the monks of St. Cuthbert from the church, in consequence of a feud which existed between himself and the bishop; and he gave it to Paul,[1] the abbot of the monastery of St. Alban the Martyr. This abbot was frequently admonished, entreated, yea, warned by the monks of Durham, not to invade another man's property; but he gave no heed—nay, he all the more pertinaciously sent his own people to reside there. Not long afterwards, he himself followed them; but he was seized with a sudden fit of illness, and as he was endeavouring to return home, he died.[2] The earl, also, lost his entire property, his honour, and his liberty, in that very church of which he had plundered St. Cuthbert.[3]

Chap. LXIV.[4]—Of the Acquisitions made by Bishop William, and how he conducted himself towards those who were under him.

This bishop William never at any time took anything from the church—nay, on the contrary, so far from doing so, his study was to add to its possessions, and to adorn it with precious ornaments of various kinds. By his energy and prudence, under God's assistance, he so defended and preserved the rights, laws, and privileges of the church, that, during his lifetime, they could neither be infringed nor violated by any person whatever. For there were certain lands respecting which there had been a constant strife between the bishop of Durham and the earl of Northumberland; and yet he left these to the church so entirely free and quit, that from that time forward no one, save the bishop alone, either ought or could demand from them any customs; and this the charters of the church prove. As a loving father deals with his sons who are dearest to him, so did he protect and cherish the monks, ruling them with the greatest discretion. Whether he chid them or praised them, he was so endeared to them all, that neither did his severity degenerate into harshness, nor his gentleness into laxity; but the one was so tempered by the other, that his severity was gentle, and his gentleness severe. He loved them much, and much did they love him. His exhortations to them were chiefly to this effect—that they should respect their habit and observe their order. This he himself took care to do constantly; when present, by his words; when absent, by his letters. This his diligence, this his anxiety, are attested by those letters of holy admonition of his which are preserved in this church, as a memorial of him, even to the present day; for when the king's affairs prevented him from visiting them personally, he despatched letters to them, some of which it may be expedient to insert in this place.

[1] See the Vitæ Vigintitrium S. Albani Abbatum, by M. Paris, p. 51, ed. fol. Lond. 1640.
[2] He died on the third of the ides of November, 1093. Id. p. 53.
[3] Robert de Mowbray was taken prisoner at Tynemouth, the particulars of which may be seen in Dugd. Monast. i. 46, and Dugd. Baron. i. 57.
[4] In Twysden's edition, book IV. chap. v.

CHAP. LXV.[1]—A LETTER OF BISHOP WILLIAM TO THE MONKS OF DURHAM.

" WILLIAM, bishop of Durham, to his brethren in Christ, and to his sons, the monks of Durham, sends greeting, and the blessing which giveth life.

" I am persuaded that you will believe me to be in earnest, when I tell you how sorry I am that I cannot tarry with you, as indeed I ought to do; but in what place soever, or in what business soever, I may be sinfully employed, my spirit turns back to you, and there finds peace and joy. My prayer is that you, for your part, would daily think upon my misfortunes, and that you would strengthen my weakness with your devout prayers and alms. Do this of your charity, and do it without grutching. This much, however, I command and entreat you; that you would increase more and more in fervent love towards your order; and on no account, under no pressure, permit your order to wane, and spare none of your number who do so. When in the church, chant the psalms and other services, not hurriedly, but decently and in order. Make confession frequently to the prior; let all attend the chapter, all without exception, save only the sick, and those persons who are regularly engaged in such business as takes them abroad. And since at this present time I cannot say to you what I should wish to do, let this letter be read once each week in the chapter, in order that you may observe more strictly what it enjoins, and recommend me to God all the more earnestly when you hear me addressing you. And since charity covereth a multitude of sins, have true charity, not only towards pilgrims and wayfarers, but also towards all sorts and conditions of men. By these, and such like good works, God will cause you to live in safety in this present life, and give you to inherit eternal glory in eternity, who liveth and reigneth for ever and ever."

CHAP. LXVI.[2]—ABOUT THE DEATH OF PRIOR ALDWIN, AND THE SUCCESSION OF TURGOT.

IN the year of our Lord's incarnation ten hundred and eighty-seven, when the fourth year of the residence of the monks in Durham had nearly come to a termination, the venerable prior Aldwin ended this present life, on the day before the ides of April [12th April], in the fourteenth year after he had first come into the province of the Northumbrians. The bishop and the brethren deeply bewailed his decease, for he was a good man and a modest; by his prudence and counsel, he was very necessary to the welfare of the church; and in whatever matter he undertook, he was exceedingly solicitous not to offend God. His merits are such as to demand that the monks of Durham shall make unceasing mention of him in their prayers; for he was their forerunner into the province, in which, guided by his example and instruction, they have become the servants of Christ. By the general advice of the brethren, the bishop appointed as his successor in the office of prior, one who had been his disciple, namely, Turgot; and enjoined

---

[1] In Twysden's edition, book IV. chap. vi.   [2] Id. book IV. chap. vii.

him to rule the whole monastery, as well within as without, in the fear of God.

In the same year in which Aldwin died, died also king William, upon the fifth of the ides of September [9th Sept.], five weeks before the completion of the twenty-second year of his reign, and left the sceptre to his son William.

CHAP. LXVII.[1]—OF THE EXILE OF BISHOP WILLIAM, AND HOW HE LAID THE FOUNDATIONS OF THE NEW MONASTERY IN DURHAM.

THE bishop of whom we have been speaking enjoyed for a time the familiar friendship of the new king, as he had previously done that of his father; so much so, indeed, that he gave him Alverton with its adjuncts.[2] But, no long period after this, a dispute arose between them, through the machinations of others;[3] and the bishop, withdrawing from his episcopate, passed the sea, and having been welcomed by the earl of Normandy, he spent the three years of his residence with him in great honour, not as an exile, but as a father. The monks of Durham, being thus deprived of the comfort of the presence of their bishop, were apprehensive that they would encounter many adversities, and that they would find no one to assist them; whereas, exactly contrary to this, they were so protected by God, through the merits of St. Cuthbert, that they were endamaged by no calamities, and found by their own experience that the king was sufficiently gentle towards them. For, although his conduct towards other monasteries and churches was ferocious, not only did he not deprive them of any portion of their property, but he even contributed to it from his own, and, like his father, defended them from the injuries of the oppressor. Moreover, when the prior came to him, he humbly arose to meet him, received him kindly, and enjoined him freely to exercise due care over the church in all things, as if he were its bishop.

At this time the monks built the refectory, as it appears at present.

In the third year of the bishop's expulsion, whilst the king's followers were being besieged within a certain castle in Normandy, of which they formed the garrison, and were just about to be taken prisoners, the bishop delivered them from the danger, and by his advice the siege was raised. Hereupon the king was pacified, and restored him all his former possessions in England. He did not return home empty-handed, but took care to despatch to the church, before he came himself, many sacred vessels for the altar, and diverse ornaments of gold and silver, as well as several books. Not long after this, he gave directions that the then existing fabric should be pulled down, in the ninety-eighth year after it had been founded by Aldhun; and in the ensuing year, he laid the founda-

---

[1] In Twysden's edition, book IV. chap. viii.

[2] See the charter printed in the Appendix to the Three Historians, p. xxii.

[3] Many additional and interesting details are given in the History of the unjust Persecution of the first Bishop William, inflicted by King William the son of the great King William, which occurs in this present volume; p. 731.

tions of a fabric much larger and more noble, which he intended to erect. It was commenced upon Thursday, the third of the ides of August [11th Aug.], in the year of our Lord's incarnation ten hundred and ninety-three, being the thirteenth year of the pontificate of the said William, and the eleventh after the monks had taken up their abode at Durham. Upon that day, the bishop and prior Turgot (who was the second in authority after the bishop in the church), and the other brethren, laid the first foundation stones. A short time before this, upon Friday, the fourth of the kalends of August [29th July], the same bishop and prior, after they had joined in prayer with the brethren, and given them their benediction, had begun to dig the foundations. There, whilst the monks were building their own offices, the bishop carried on the works of the church at his own expense. At the same time he led forth the said prior Turgot, in the presence of the population of the whole episcopate, and delegated to him his authority over them, to this effect,—that, taking upon him the office of the archdeaconry, he should thereby have the charge of the Christianity of the entire diocese; and he further decided, that all those who succeeded him in the office of prior should also be his successor in that of the archdeaconry. This he did not do without authority and precedent; for we read in the Life of St. Cuthbert,[1] that when the blessed Boisil was provost of the monastery, it was his constant custom to go out of it and to preach to the people. On his decease, his blessed disciple—Cuthbert, I mean,—succeeded him in the office of provost, which is the same as that of prior; for the individual whom we now style prior is called "provost of the monastery" by the blessed Benedict.[2] So the father Cuthbert imitated the example of his master, and was in the frequent habit of leaving the monastery, and not returning to it sometimes for a whole week, sometimes for two or even three, and occasionally for an entire month; but he remained in the mountainous districts, by his preaching and powerful example calling the rustic population to think of heavenly things. Hence the bishop was induced to make the arrangement, that whosoever should succeed St. Cuthbert in the church by filling the office of prior, should in like manner discharge the functions of a preacher, and take charge of the Christianity of the see.

CHAP. LXVIII.[3]—OF THE VISION OF A KNIGHT NAMED BOSO, RESPECTING THE MONKS OF DURHAM; AND OF HIS PREDICTIONS CONCERNING THE DECEASE OF BISHOP WILLIAM.

AT this time there was one of the bishop's knights, named Boso, who, having been attacked with sickness, appeared to be at his last gasp; for there was only the slightest possible breathing from his mouth and nostrils during the three days in which he lay senseless, and like a dead man removed from the world; but, to the surprise of all, he returned to himself upon the third day. He said that he

---

[1] See chap. ix. § 15 of that work.
[2] Regula S. Benedicti, capp. lxiv. lxv.
[3] In Twysden's edition, book IV. chap. ix.

had seen many visions, but did not mention the details to any person until he had made the prior acquainted with their import, as, indeed, he had been commanded to do. So soon as he had regained his strength, he came to the prior in haste, and requested that he might have the opportunity of conversing with him in private. There he cast aside his garments, and fell at his feet, naked, carrying some rods in his hands; and then he exclaimed, with tears: "I am commanded to come to you, and to confess my sins to you, and to rule my life—which, however, will not be long—according to your directions. I entreat you, therefore, to receive my penance; and, through the medium of these stripes, convey healing to the wounds inflicted by my sins, that so I may escape the strictness of the future judgment of God." So he confessed his sins with many lamentations; and when he had received the penance, he recounted the narrative which follows:—

"I followed the guide, who led me through various places, of which some were terrible and some were pleasant. All the monks of this church were congregated in one spot, and before them was carried a cross worthy of veneration, from which a bright light emanated; and it was followed by all the monks in their vestments, singing, in solemn and regular procession, as is their usual custom. They all advanced in a regular order, without any deviation either to the right hand or the left, excepting two of their number only, who slightly diverged from the column; and the whole of this procession kept steadily advancing towards an exceedingly lofty wall which was opposite to them, and in which there was not the slightest appearance of either door or window. When I was meditating in my own mind, and wondering for what purpose they were going thither, since there was no entrance there, suddenly they all, I know not how, were inside the wall. I, however, was still on the outside, and looked round me, in the hope of noticing some mode of discovering what was passing inside; and at the last I perceived a very small window. Looking through it, I saw a field of considerable extent, beautiful by the variety of blooming flowers with which it was clad, and from which were exhaled odours of the most wonderful fragrance. My guide inquired if I could recognise who those persons were who were inside; and my reply was, that I had discovered that they were our own monks. He answered: 'Tell the prior to exhort them to the more diligent care of their souls; and specify to him by name who those two persons were, who, as you observed, left the column of the procession; for of a truth they are wandering not a little from the path of righteousness, and there is an especial necessity why they should make a cleaner confession of their sins, and hasten to lead a life of greater strictness; for hitherto they have never made a true and full confession of their sins.' So he led me to where I could observe all the inhabitants of this province assembled in a field of immense extent; they were mounted upon very fat horses, and (according to their usual custom) were carrying long spears; and as they tilted with these the one against the other, the shivering of the lances occasioned a considerable noise, and the riders swelled with pride.

Hereupon my guide asked me if I knew who these persons were; and my reply was, that I recognised first one, then another; and, lastly, that I could distinguish every single individual of their number. Whereupon he added, 'All these persons are on the very verge of destruction;' and immediately as he spoke the words, the whole multitude vanished away like smoke from before my eyes.

" They were next succeeded by a body of Frenchmen, far prouder than those who had gone before them: they, too, were mounted on foaming horses, and clothed in armour of every kind; and the neighing of their steeds, and the clashing of their armour, made a noise which extended far and wide.   But after a short while, they and all their glory were swallowed up by the earth, which opened her mouth, and no trace of them appeared.   Casting my eyes over the field once more, I saw it covered, for some miles, with a large body of women; and while I was in astonishment at their number, my guide informed me that they were the wives of priests.   He spoke thus: 'These wretched women, and those persons also who were consecrated for sacrificing to God, but who, unworthy, have become enchained in the pleasures of the flesh, are awaiting the eternal sentence of condemnation, and the severe punishment of the fires of hell.'

" Next I looked upon a dwelling-place of great loftiness, framed entirely of iron; it stood alone in a horrid wilderness, and the entrance to it was constantly being opened and closed; and bishop William, suddenly putting forth his head, inquired of me where was the monk Gosfrid. ' For,' said he, ' it was his duty to be here with me at the trial.'   The bishop had appointed this man as his procurator.   Then my guide said to me: ' You may know of a truth that the end of the bishop's life is close at hand, and the person for whom he is inquiring will follow him no very long time after. And as for yourself, since you are permitted for a little space longer to live in the world, endeavour to escape God's wrath, and, after having confessed your sins, study how to lead a life in accordance with the instructions which you will receive from the prior; and have no hesitation in making him fully acquainted with all that has been manifested to you."

This knight stated that he had seen and heard these things which we have reported, and others also; and their truthfulness was shortly afterwards established by the death, as well of the bishop as of those various other persons whose departure had been predicted. And those two brethren, who were observed as having departed from the line of the procession, also bore witness to the truth of his words; for the prior, having made a careful investigation into their lives, discovered the accuracy of the statement which the knight had made to him in private.

CHAP. LXIX.[1]—OF THE PLACE WHERE BISHOP WILLIAM DIED, AND HOW HIS
BODY WAS CONVEYED TO DURHAM.

Now, while this knight, at the command of the prior, recounted to the bishop the narrative of his vision, the latter trembled and

[1] In Twysden's edition, book IV. chap. x.

was in great terror when he heard it; and from that time forth he took the greater care of his [soul's] health; he was more profuse in his alms, longer and more intent in his devotions, nor would he omit his stated daily prayers to attend to any business whatever. And, of a truth, for a long while before his decease, his health had been very infirm; but he was seized with a sharper attack than usual one Christmas-day,[1] which he was spending at Windsor, and he struggled with the disease, which was fatal to him, for eight days. In the meantime, many persons visited him; some to ask him for his advice in their necessities, for he was a man of great skill; some to comfort the sick man with words of holy consolation. The chief agent in this work was Anselm, the venerable archbishop of Canterbury, whose private exhortation respecting his soul's health the bishop long enjoyed, and rejoiced that he had derived from him the grace of consolation and blessing. Worn out with this infirmity, he had no longer a more earnest desire for life than he had for death; but his most urgent prayer to God was this—that whatever He knew to be best for him, He would vouchsafe to grant him, whether it were a longer life or present death. But upon the evening of the eighth day, being the festival of the Circumcision, when the nearer approach of death showed that the sentence was irrevocable, he asked that he might participate in the comforts of those who depart in the faith; these offices were administered to him with the greatest devoutness (after having made a confession of the catholic faith) by the hands of Thomas, the archbishop of York, of venerable memory, assisted by Walkeline, bishop of Winchester, and John, bishop of Bath. To these prelates he committed himself and his children, that is, the monks of this church; and he anxiously strove how to recommend them to their care and protection. Whilst he was thus awaiting the hour of his summons, the bishops were deliberating as to the place in which he should be buried; and it appeared to them to be most expedient and most fitting that his body should be interred within the church of St. Cuthbert, for he had always been most anxious that the holy body of that bishop and confessor should have a continual service, worthy and pleasing to God, performed by a congregation of monks established in that spot. But he protested against this arrangement, and earnestly forbade it. "By no means," said he, "by no means let my dead body be the occasion of that custom of the church of the holy Cuthbert being broken, which has been so carefully preserved from the remotest period up to this present hour: for never has the corpse of any one been introduced, even for an hour, within the place in which his incorrupt body reposes, much less been there buried." They decided, therefore, that he should be interred in the chapter-house, since it was a locality in which the brethren, having to assemble therein daily,[2] would be daily reminded in their hearts of their dearly beloved father, by the sight of his tomb.

The disease now became more severe with the bishop, and the

---

[1] A.D. 1095.
[2] Upon the assembly of the monks in the chapter-house, see Martene, De Antiq. Monachorum Ritibus, I. v. § 3.

pallor of death came upon him; and so he ended his life near upon the hour of cock-crowing, upon the fourth of the nones of January [2d Jan. 1096], being the fourth day of the week. According to the established custom, his body was clothed in his vestments, and the brethren who were present conveyed it to Durham. The monks, the clerks, and the whole population met it, and removed it with much sorrow and lamentation, and carried it into the church of St. Michael. Therein its obsequies were performed the first night by the clergy and the people; but on the morning, the monks taking the body into their own possession, passed that day and the following night in prayers, in the chanting of psalms, and in watching. On the ensuing day, that is, on the seventeenth of the kalends of February [16th Jan.], they committed it, with the honour which was its due, to the grave, in the spot which the bishops had selected, as we have already mentioned. How great was their grief for the loss of so good a father, how deep their sorrow, how bitter their tears, it is better in my opinion to pass over in silence, than to make a statement which to some persons might appear to be incredible. But I am persuaded, that of all those present there was not one who would not have recalled the bishop to life, could he have done so at the cost of his own. He died in the year of our Lord's incarnation one thousand and ninety-six, after having spent fifteen years and two months, all but three days, in the bishopric; and this occurred in the thirteenth year after the monks had taken up their abode in Durham.

HERE ENDS SIMEON'S HISTORY.

SIMEON'S ACCOUNT OF THE SIEGE OF DURHAM.

IN the year of our Lord's incarnation nine hundred and sixty-nine, during the reign of Ethelred, king of the English, Malcolm, king of the Scots, the son of king Kyned, collected together the entire military force of Scotland; and having devastated the province of the Northumbrians with the sword and fire, he laid siege to Durham. At this time bishop Aldun had the government there; for Waltheof, who was the earl of the Northumbrians, had shut himself up in Bebbanburc [Bamborough]. He was exceedingly aged, and in consequence could not undertake any active measures against the enemy. Bishop Aldun had given his daughter, named Ecgfrida, in marriage to Cospatric's son, named Ucthred, a youth of great energy, and well skilled in military affairs; and along with her the bishop had given him these vills—part of the lands of St. Cuthbert, namely, Bermetun, Skirningheim, Eltun, Carltun, Heaclif, and Heseldene, upon these terms, namely, that so long as he lived, he would treat his wife with honour.

Now, when this young man perceived that the land was devastated by the enemy, and that Durham was in a state of blockade and siege, he collected together into one body a considerable number of the men of Northumbria and Yorkshire, and cut to pieces nearly the entire multitude of the Scots; the king himself, and a few others, escaping with difficulty. He caused to be carried to Durham the best-looking heads of the slain, ornamented (as the fashion of the time was) with braided locks, and after they had been washed by four women,—to each of whom he gave a cow for her trouble,—he caused these heads to be fixed upon stakes, and placed round about the walls.

When king Ethelred heard of this, he summoned this young man to his presence (this was during the lifetime of his father Waltheof,) and as a reward for his courage, and for the battle which he had fought so gallantly, he gave him the earldom which had been his father's, adding thereto the earldom of the men of York. Upon his return home, however, Ucthred sent away the daughter of bishop Aldun; and because in so doing he had acted contrary to his promise and oath, the father of the young woman (I mean, the bishop) took back to the church the lands which he had given Ucthred, along with his daughter. Having thus put away the bishop's daughter, as we have mentioned, Ucthred took to wife the daughter of a rich citizen, named Styr, the son of Ulf, (her name

¹ From Twysden's edition, col. 79.

was Sigen); and her father gave her to him upon the understanding that he would put to death Turbrand, who was most hostile towards himself (Styr). Afterwards, when Ucthred had made additional progress in military affairs, king Ethelred gave him his own daughter Elfgiva in marriage; by whom he had Algitha, whom her father wedded to Maldred, the son of Crinan the thane; by whom Maldred became the father of Cospatric, who begat Dolphin, and Waltheof, and Cospatric. The daughter of bishop Aldun, whom earl Ucthred had sent away, became the wife of a certain thane in Yorkshire, namely, Kilvert, the son of Ligulf; their daughter, Sigrida, became the wife of Arkil, the son of Ecgfrid, and she bore him a son named Cospatric. This Cospatric took to wife the daughter of Dolfin, the son of Torfin, by whom he begot Cospatric, who of late ought to have fought with Waltheof, the son of Eilaf. Kilvert, the son of Ligulf, sent away the daughter of bishop Aldun, (I mean, Ecgfrida,) whereupon her father commanded her to return forthwith to Durham; and when she obeyed his commands, she brought back with her Bermetun, and Skirningheim, and Eltun, which she had retained in her own possession; and thus she restored to the church and the bishop the lands which properly belonged to them. After this she took the veil, which she kept faithfully until the day of her death: she lies buried in the churchyard of Durham, awaiting the day of judgment.

In order to detail the death of earl Ucthred, our narrative must revert a little. Suein, the king of the Danes, having driven Ethelred, the king of the English, into Normandy, took possession of his realm; but upon his death, which occurred no long time afterwards, king Ethelred returned to his own kingdom, having taken to wife Emma, the daughter of Richard, the duke of the Normans. Only a very short time had elapsed, when Cnut, the son of Suein, the king of the Danes, whom we have already mentioned, came to England, accompanied by a countless multitude, meaning to reign over it. He sent a message to Ucthred, asking him to join him, along with all the men whom he could muster, to render him assistance against king Ethelred; promising him that, in the event of his compliance, not only should he retain possession of the honour which he then held, but that something yet more extensive should be added. This earl was a man of considerable influence, for he had under him the counties of Northumberland and York. Ucthred, however, answered that he would do nothing of the sort, and declared that it would be the depth of baseness were he to act thus against his lord and father-in-law. "Nothing would induce me," said he, "to take such a step: nor, indeed, ought I to do so. So long as king Ethelred lives, I will be faithful to him; for he is my lord and my wife's father, and the abundant honours and riches which are mine, I possess by his gift. I will never be a traitor to him." Thus Cnut had no assistance from Ucthred.

But upon the death of Ethelred, when Cnut became possessed of the whole realm of England, he sent a message to the earl, commanding that he would come to him as his lord. Having received a safe-conduct for his journey there and home again, the earl went,

Upon the day appointed, as he was going to the king to treat of peace, certain of the king's armed soldiers, who were hidden within the traverse of the house at Wiheal, behind a curtain which was there suspended, suddenly rushed out and killed the earl, and forty of the chiefest of his men, who had entered along with him. This was planned by the treachery of a certain powerful man, Turebrant, surnamed Hold.

Upon his death, his brother Eadulf, surnamed Cudel, a lazy and cowardly fellow, succeeded him in the earldom. Apprehensive that the Scots would revenge upon himself the slaughter which his brother had inflicted upon them, as has been already mentioned, he yielded up to' them the whole of Lothian, to soothe them and procure a peace; and hence it is that Lothian became added to the kingdom of Scotland. But Eadulf having died shortly after this, Aldred—whom the aforesaid Ucthred had begotten by Ecfrid, the daughter of bishop Aldun, of whom we have already made mention, —became possessed of the earldom of Northumberland only, and put to death Turebrant, who had murdered his father. Carl, the son of this Turebrant, and earl Aldred were engaged in a mutual enmity, and were constantly laying traps the one for the other; but at last, by the agency of their friends, they were brought to an agreement; by whose instrumentality also they made satisfaction to each other. So firmly knit, indeed, was their friendship, that, like sworn brethren, they meant to visit Rome together; but a long-continued tempest of the sea hindered them, and they were constrained to abandon their plan, and return homewards. Carl received the earl into his house with great pomp and due respect; but, after having provided an entertainment for him, and when he was entirely thrown off his guard, he conducted him, as if out of compliment, into the wood called Risewude, and there he slew him, when he suspected no harm. A little cross of stone marks, even to this day, the spot at which he was murdered. Earl Waltheof, the grandson of earl Aldred,—for he was the son of his daughter,—some time afterwards avenged the death of his grandfather with a mighty slaughter; for which purpose he had collected a large assembly of young men. For when the sons of Carl were feasting together in the house of their elder brother, at Seteringeton, not far from York, the party which had been despatched there for that purpose fell upon them unawares, and put the whole of them to death, with the sole exception of Cnut, whose life was spared from regard to his innate excellence of disposition. Sumerlede, who is alive at this present day, happened not to be there. Having massacred the sons and grandsons of Carl, they returned, carrying with them many and diverse spoils. But we must now return to the point from which we digressed.

Earl Aldred was the father of five daughters, three of whom bore the same name, Aelfleda; the fourth was called Aldgitha, and the fifth Etheldritha. One of these Aelfledas married earl Siward, by whom she became the mother of Waltheof; and as this Aelfleda was countess,—being the daughter of earl Aldred, and he the son of earl Ucthred and the daughter of bishop Aldun,—she laid claim to these lands following, as belonging to her by hereditary right; namely, Bernetun, Kyrningeim, Eltun, Carltun, Heaclif, and Heseldene, which earl Siward her husband had given her; and she gave to her son Waltheof the earldom of Northumberland, as it had been held by Waltheof's grandfather, earl Aldred.

Upon the death of earl Siward and the countess Alfleda, the daughter of earl Aldred, a war broke out, in consequence of which that land was devastated. After a long time, that Arkil, the son of Ecgfrid, already mentioned, (who had taken to wife Sigrida, the daughter of Kilvert and of Ecgfrida, the daughter of bishop Aldun,) possessed himself of these lands, which had been thus devastated, and they settled upon them. Upon the death of his wife Sigrida, he gave not only Heseldene to St. Cuthbert, but also Heaclif and Carltun, which are still in the possession of the church. Arkil the son of Fridegist, and earl Eadulf, and Arkil the son of Ecgfrith, these three had Sigrida [to wife]. Afterwards, when king William came into England, this Arkil took to flight, and became a banished man; and thus for the second time this land continued devastated. After these occurrences, a certain thane of Yorkshire, called Orm, the son of Gamel, took to wife Etheldritha, one of the five daughters of earl Aldred; and she bare to him a daughter named Ecgfrida, who, by Eilsi of Tees, became the mother of Waltheof, and his two brothers, and Eda their sister. And as that Ecgfrida was descended from earl Aldred and the daughter of bishop Aldun, she—that is, Ecgfrida—and her husband Eilsi, took possession of Bermetun and Skirningheim by hereditary right.

Also published by Llanerch:

A HISTORY OF THE KINGS OF ENGLAND
by Simeon of Durham.

LIFE OF ST. COLUMBA
by Adamnan.

A HISTORY OF THE KINGS OF ENGLAND
by Florence of Worcester.

CONTEMPORARY CHRONICLES
OF THE MIDDLE AGES
by William of Malmesbury,
Richard of Hexham,
and Jordan Fantosme.

MEDIAEVAL CHRONICLES OF SCOTLAND
The Chronicles of Melrose, and Holyrood.

THE MYSTICAL WAY
AND THE ARTHURIAN QUEST
by Derek Bryce.

THE CELTIC LEGEND OF THE BEYOND
by F. M. Luzel.

From booksellers. Write to the publishers
for a complete list:
Llanerch Enterprises, Felinfach,
Lampeter, Dyfed, Wales.
SA48 8PJ.